Move

33 1/3 Global

33 1/3 Global, a series related to but independent from **33 1/3**, takes the format of the original series of short, music-based books and brings the focus to music throughout the world. With initial volumes focusing on Japanese and Brazilian music, the series will also include volumes on the popular music of Australia/Oceania, Europe, Africa, the Middle East, and more.

33 1/3 Japan

Series Editor: Noriko Manabe

Spanning a range of artists and genres—from the 1970s rock of Happy End to technopop band Yellow Magic Orchestra, the Shibuya-kei of Cornelius, classic anime series *Cowboy Bebop*, J-Pop/EDM hybrid Perfume, and vocaloid star Hatsune Miku—33 1/3 Japan is a series devoted to in-depth examination of Japanese popular music of the twentieth and twenty-first centuries.

Published Titles:
Supercell's *Supercell* by Keisuke Yamada
AKB48 by Patrick W. Galbraith and Jason G. Karlin
Yoko Kanno's *Cowboy Bebop Soundtrack* by Rose Bridges
Perfume's *Game* by Patrick St. Michel
Cornelius's *Fantasma* by Martin Roberts
Joe Hisaishi's *My Neighbor Totoro: Soundtrack* by Kunio Hara
Shonen Knife's *Happy Hour* by Brooke McCorkle
Nenes's *Koza Dabasa* by Henry Johnson
Yuming's *The 14th Moon* by Lasse Lehtonen
Toshiko Akiyoshi-Lew Tabackin Big Band's *Kogun* by E. Taylor Atkins
S.O.B.'s *Don't Be Swindle* by Mahon Murphy and Ran Zwigenberg

Forthcoming Titles:
Kohaku Utagassen: The Red and White Song Contest by Shelley Brunt
Yellow Magic Orchestra's *Yellow Magic Orchestra* by Toshiyuki Ohwada

33 1/3 Brazil

Series Editor: Jason Stanyek

Covering the genres of samba, tropicália, rock, hip hop, forró, bossa nova, heavy metal and funk, among others, 33 1/3 Brazil is a series devoted to in-depth examination of the most important Brazilian albums of the twentieth and twenty-first centuries.

Published Titles:

Caetano Veloso's *A Foreign Sound* by Barbara Browning

Tim Maia's *Tim Maia Racional Vols. 1 & 2* by Allen Thayer

João Gilberto and Stan Getz's *Getz/Gilberto* by Brian McCann

Gilberto Gil's *Refazenda* by Marc A. Hertzman

Dona Ivone Lara's *Sorriso Negro* by Mila Burns

Milton Nascimento and Lô Borges's *The Corner Club* by Jonathon Grasse

Racionais MCs' *Sobrevivendo no Inferno* by Derek Pardue

Naná Vasconcelos's *Saudades* by Daniel B. Sharp

Chico Buarque's *First Chico Buarque* by Charles A. Perrone

Forthcoming Titles:

Jorge Ben Jor's *África Brasil* by Frederick J. Moehn

33 1/3 Europe

Series Editor: Fabian Holt

Spanning a range of artists and genres, 33 1/3 Europe offers engaging accounts of popular and culturally significant albums of Continental Europe and the North Atlantic from the twentieth and twenty-first centuries.

Published Titles:

Darkthrone's *A Blaze in the Northern Sky* by Ross Hagen

Ivo Papazov's *Balkanology* by Carol Silverman

Heiner Müller and Heiner Goebbels's *Wolokolamsker Chaussee* by Philip V. Bohlman

Modeselektor's *Happy Birthday!* by Sean Nye

Mercyful Fate's *Don't Break the Oath* by Henrik Marstal

Bea Playa's *I'll Be Your Plaything* by Anna Szemere and András Rónai
Various Artists' *DJs do Guetto* by Richard Elliott
Czesław Niemen's *Niemen Enigmatic* by Ewa Mazierska and Mariusz Gradowski
Massada's *Astaganaga* by Lutgard Mutsaers
Los Rodriguez's *Sin Documentos* by Fernán del Val and Héctor Fouce
Édith Piaf's *Récital 1961* by David Looseley
Nuovo Canzoniere Italiano's *Bella Ciao* by Jacopo Tomatis
Iannis Xenakis's *Persepolis* by Aram Yardumian
Vopli Vidopliassova's *Tantsi* by Maria Sonevytsky
Amália Rodrigues's *Amália at the Olympia* by Lila Ellen Gray
Ardit Gjebrea's *Projekt Jon* by Nicholas Tochka
Aqua's *Aquarium* by C.C. McKee
J.M.K.E.'s *To the Cold Land* by Brigitta Davidjants
Taco Hemingway's *Jarmark* by Kamila Rymajdo
Einstürzende Neubauten's *Kollaps* by Melle Jan Kromhout and Jan Nieuwenhuis
CCCP – FEDELI ALLA LINEA's *Affinità – Divergenze Fra il Compagno Togliatti e Noi* by Giacomo Bottà
Silly's *Februar* by Michael Rauhut

Forthcoming Titles:
Sigur Rós' *Ágætis Byrjun* by Tore Størvold
Aphrodite's Child's *666* by Ana Leorne

33 1/3 Oceania

Series Editors: Jon Stratton (senior editor) and Jon Dale (specializing in books on albums from Aotearoa/New Zealand)
Spanning a range of artists and genres from Australian Indigenous artists to Maori and Pasifika artists, from Aotearoa/New Zealand noise music to Australian rock, and including music from Papua and other Pacific islands, 33 1/3 Oceania offers exciting accounts of albums that illustrate the wide range of music made in the Oceania region.

Published Titles:
John Farnham's *Whispering Jack* by Graeme Turner
The Church's *Starfish* by Chris Gibson

Regurgitator's *Unit* by Lachlan Goold and Lauren Istvandity

Kylie Minogue's *Kylie* by Adrian Renzo and Liz Giuffre

Alastair Riddell's *Space Waltz* by Ian Chapman

Hunters & Collectors's *Human Frailty* by Jon Stratton

The Front Lawn's *Songs from the Front Lawn* by Matthew Bannister

Bic Runga's *Drive* by Henry Johnson

The Dead C's *Clyma est mort* by Darren Jorgensen

Ed Kuepper's *Honey Steel's Gold* by John Encarnacao

Chain's *Toward the Blues* by Peter Beilharz

Hilltop Hoods' *The Calling* by Dianne Rodger

Screamfeeder's *Kitten Licks* by Ben Green and Ian Rogers

The Clean's *Boodle Boodle Boodle* by Geoff Stahl

The Avalanches' *Since I Left You* by Charles Fairchild

John Sangster's *Lord of the Rings Vols. 1–3* by Bruce Johnson

Soundtrack from *Saturday Night Fever* by Clinton Walker

Eyeliner's *BUY NOW* by Michael Brown

TISM's *Machiavelli and the Four Seasons* by Tyler Jenke

Crowded House's *Together Alone* by Barnaby Smith

silverchair's *Frogstomp* by Jay Daniel Thompson

Various Artists' *Truckload of Sky: The Lost Songs of David McComb* by Glenn D'Cruz

Robert Forster's *Danger in the Past* by Patrick Chapman

Tame Impala's *Currents* by Alister Newstead

The Three Out's *Move* by James Gaunt

Forthcoming Titles:

The Triffids' *Born Sandy Devotional* by Christina Ballico

5MMM's *Compilation Album of Adelaide Bands 1980* by Collette Snowden

INXS' *Kick* by Lauren Moxey

Sunnyboys' *Sunnyboys* by Stephen Bruel

The La De Da's *The Happy Prince* by John Tebbutt

Gary Shearston's *Dingo* by Peter Mills

Kate Ceberano's *Brave* by Panizza Allmark

Dinah Lee's *Introducing Dinah Lee* by Kimberly Cannady

The Waifs' *Up All Night* by Rebecca Bennison

Split Enz' *Mental Notes* by Michael Lamb

Douglas Lilburn's *Complete Electro-Acoustic Works* by Bruce Russell
Savage Garden's *Affirmation* by Pat O'Grady
Dick Diver's *Calendar Days* by Mitch Ryan
Blood Duster's *Fisting the Dead* by Rosemary Overell
Olivia Newton-John's *Physical* by Jarrod Sturnieks
Stella Donnelly's *Beware of the Dogs* by Emily Wilson

33 1/3 South Asia

Series Editor: Natalie Sarrazin

From the films of Bollywood and Lollywood, to home-grown *bhangra* hip-hop, Hindu devotional pop and Sufi rock, Sri Lankan rap, Indo jazz and disco, new-wave electronica and diasporic Asian Underground scene, 33 1/3 South Asia takes readers on a sonically diverse journey through the most significant soundtracks and albums from the twentieth and twenty-first centuries.

Published Titles:

Dil Chahta Hai Soundtrack by Jayson Beaster-Jones
Lata Mangeshkar's *My Favourites, Volume 2* by Anirudha Bhattacharjee and Chandrashekhar Rao
Coke Studio (Season 14) by Rakae Rehman Jamil and Khadija Muzaffar

33 1/3 Africa

Series Editor: Michael Veal

33 1/3 Africa is a series of books on canonical, album-length works of African music including traditional music, experimental music, and, with particular emphasis, popular music. Academic and journalistic writing results in sophisticated, nuanced and accessible narratives on African music.

Published Titles:

Fela Anikulapo-Kuti's *Sorrow Tears and Blood* by Stephanie Shonekan

Forthcoming Titles:

Cesária Évora's *Miss Perfumado* by Jacqueline Georgis
Paul Simon's *Graceland* by Kalvin Schmidt-Rimpler Dinh
Nico, Rochereau, Roger & L'African Fiesta – *Volume 1 (1962–1963)* by Frank Gunderson

Move

James Gaunt

Series Editor: Jon Stratton, UniSA Creative, University of South Australia, and Jon Dale, University of Melbourne, Australia

BLOOMSBURY ACADEMIC
NEW YORK • LONDON • OXFORD • NEW DELHI • SYDNEY

BLOOMSBURY ACADEMIC
Bloomsbury Publishing Inc, 1359 Broadway, New York, NY 10018, USA
Bloomsbury Publishing Plc, 50 Bedford Square, London, WC1B 3DP, UK
Bloomsbury Publishing Ireland, 29 Earlsfort Terrace, Dublin 2, D02 AY28, Ireland

BLOOMSBURY, BLOOMSBURY ACADEMIC and the Diana logo are
trademarks of Bloomsbury Publishing Plc

First published in the United States of America 2026

Bloomsbury Publishing Inc does not have any control over, or responsibility
for, any third-party websites referred to or in this book. All internet addresses
given in this book were correct at the time of going to press. The author and
publisher regret any inconvenience caused if addresses have changed or sites
have ceased to exist, but can accept no responsibility for any such changes.

A catalog record for this book is available from the Library of Congress.

ISBN: HB: 979-8-7651-2296-9
         PB: 979-8-7651-2297-6
         ePDF: 979-8-7651-2299-0
         eBook: 979-8-7651-2298-3

Series: 33 1/3 Oceania

Typeset by Integra Software Services Pvt. Ltd.
Printed and bound in the United States of America

For product safety related questions contact productsafety@bloomsbury.com.

To find out more about our authors and books visit www.bloomsbury.com
and sign up for our newsletters.

Contents

Preface x

1 **Introducing The Three Out** 1

2 **Jazz in Melbourne and Sydney** 21

3 **Moving up: The Three Out** 33

4 **Moving out: The impact of *Move*** 53

5 **The end of The Three Out** 67

6 ***Move*: An annotated bibliography and discography** 83

7 ***Move* reissued** 89

8 **Moving on** 97

Bibliography 101
Index 132

Preface

The Three Out trio were Australia's most popular modern jazz group in 1960. Made up of Dutch bassist Freddy Logan, New Zealand pianist Mike Nock, and Australian percussionist Chris Karan, they formed at the El Rocco jazz club in Sydney and recorded two albums together when few other Australian jazz albums were being recorded at all. Of the two, it's their debut *Move* that brought them to my attention and has resulted in this book.

When I first listened to *Move*, I was struck by how it compared to other Australian jazz from the 1950s and 1960s. I don't think there's anything else like it, as *Move* sounds more like the American jazz ensembles from that period led by Oscar Peterson or Miles Davis, than the Australian jazz I'd previously heard.

To better understand where this album came from, I spoke with Mike Nock and Chris Karan, as well as Brian and Mary Caddy, who shared stories of their brother-in-law Freddy Logan, who unfortunately passed away in 2003. They each discussed what The Three Out meant to them, and along the way I spoke to others who performed with them, sat in the audience listening or heard them on their turntable. Everyone told me how exciting The Three Out were as performers, and how important each member had been to the local scene.

Australian jazz of that period wasn't always recorded. There were many jazz performances in clubs, on radio and on television, from talented musicians who we will never get to hear because of this. Thankfully, The Three Out left two albums, and one live recording that has turned up along the way, so we can experience the excitement described by so many who heard them when they first appeared on the scene.

The modern jazz The Three Out performed hadn't originated in Sydney, or indeed Australia. It took inspiration from musicians from around the world who inspired each member of the trio at the beginnings of their careers. Much of that inspiration came from the United States, where jazz originated in New Orleans around the turn of the twentieth century (Mandel, 2019, p. 10). Early performances and recordings by Black American musicians such as trombonist Kid Ory, trumpeter Louis Armstrong and pianist Duke Ellington became popular around the world and jazz evolved into different subgenres, including Dixieland, Swing, Bebop, Hardbop, Free Jazz, Cool Jazz, Latin Jazz and more (Mandel, 2019, pp. 12–13, 27, 32, 252). Of those, the term 'Modern Jazz' is generally used interchangeably with Bebop. But what jazz music is and isn't can be different to different people (Whiteoak, 1998, p. 238). In researching the evolution of jazz across several countries it's clear that what was thought of as 'modern jazz' in Australia didn't always align with the trends overseas (Hentoff, 1955).

Regardless of what style of jazz you call it, *Move* was extremely well received within Australia when it was released in 1961 and it has gained fans around the world, thanks no doubt to the international reputation of the members of the trio in their later careers. For Logan his recordings with Tubby Hayes continue to be released to the approval of English jazz fans (Kenny, 2025), while Karan's soundtrack work with Roy Budd is highly celebrated (Vinyl Vulture, 2006), and each new album from Mike Nock, such as 2023's *Hearing* (Shand, 2023), brings a deluge of praise as he nears his eighty-fifth birthday. For anyone interested in these recordings, *Move* was the beginning as it featured some of the trio's first compositions. And while it remains unavailable digitally, in 2015 *Move* finally saw release on CD and was heard by new ears and remembered fondly by those who had worn out their vinyl records. So, if you haven't already, I strongly suggest finding a copy and listening to it before, during and after reading this book, as you will gain a greater appreciation for where *Move* came from and why it remains an important album for Australian jazz.

1 Introducing The Three Out

To properly tell the story of The Three Out's origins, we need to go back some thirty years before *Move* was recorded. Each member began their jazz careers in separate countries as part of different jazz scenes, and as the eldest member, The Three Out's story begins with Freddy Logan in Europe.

Freddy Logan: Jazz in the Netherlands and England

Frederik Christiaan Loggen (Amsterdam City Archives, n.d.) was born 8 April 1930 in Amsterdam, Netherlands (Oxley, 2003). He eventually shortened and anglicized his name to Fred Christian Logan (Oxley, 2003), though was also known as Freddy or Freddie for much of his career, depending on who wrote his name.

Growing up in Amsterdam, the Loggen family experienced the Second World War firsthand when Germany invaded the Netherlands in 1940. Many Dutch Jewish families were sent to concentration camps (Beek, n.d.) and the Loggen family were among those who hid Jewish children from Nazis in their cellar (Oxley, 2003). Political prisoners and opponents were also sent to camps (Netherlands Institute for War Documentation, 2024). These included Logan's younger brother Jan Loggen, who spent time in a labour camp in Hersbruck, Germany (Nationaal Archief, n.d.).

During the occupation, jazz performances had been banned across the Netherlands due to jazz's connection to Black Americans (Nederlands Jazz Archief, n.d.a). But local musicians picked up illegal broadcasts from the BBC and American Forces Network which kept them up to date with the latest music (van de Leur, 2018, p. 178). Jazz had been enjoyed across the Netherlands since the 1920s, after the Dutch dance teacher James Meyer visited London and heard The Original Dixieland Jazz Band, an American group of white musicians from New Orleans who made the first jazz records. Meyer brought this early style of jazz back to the Netherlands and began his own group. Others soon followed and there were many popular local groups such as The Ramblers, who formed in 1926 and released several gramophone records from 1929. Black American jazz musicians also visited the Netherlands including saxophonists Sidney Bechet, Benny Carter and Coleman Hawkins (Nederlands Jazz Archief, n.d.b). The Ramblers recorded with Hawkins when he spent time in the Netherlands until the advent of war (Hawkins & Ramblers, 1968).

Although jazz had been banned during the Netherlands's occupation, when Allied forces arrived in the Netherlands in May 1945 they found a thriving jazz scene with local bands ready to perform out in the open again. These included The Ramblers (Nederlands Jazz Archief, n.d.a) and others such as The Millers, who had continued to perform during the occupation (Beck, 1982, pp. 18–22). Following the country's liberation, jazz was once again popular amongst teenagers (van de Leur, 2018, p. 180), including Freddy Logan, whose interest in the double bass first started after seeing it played at a school dance in 1945. As he later recalled:

> While the band was out of the hall having a smoko, I began plucking the strings of a double bass and liked the deep sound so much that I decided I wanted to learn … I had some money left to me by my father, but as I could not touch it until I was 21 I had to apply to a law court for special permission to buy a double bass. The judge was very reluctant to give me any money when he learned that I wanted to become a professional musician and suggested that I learn a trade instead. I had to apply four times and it was six months before he agreed.
>
> (Anon., 1958)

After finally being allowed to buy a bass of his own, Logan played in several local jazz bands and became a full-time musician in 1948 (Anon., 1958). That year, he led a six-piece band at the eleventh Swing Society Festival, with Dutch newspaper *De Zaanlander* writing that his group 'brought a worthy Bebop style' (De Zaanlander van Dinsdag, 1948). Bebop was the newest jazz style following Swing which had been popular during the 1930s into the 1940s (Mandel, 2019, pp. 258–9).

Bebop was initially dismissed by some for its fast and often abrasive melodies (Mandel, 2019, p. 262). It was also set apart due to the size of the bands. While a Swing orchestra could include twenty musicians or more (Mandel, 2019, pp. 258–9), bebop groups were smaller (Gitler, 1985, p. 4). For example, early recordings of trumpeter Dizzy Gillespie's 'Salt Peanuts' were made in 1945 with a sextet and quartet (Lord, 1993, p. G201). These recordings, alongside others by saxophonists Coleman

Hawkins and Charlie 'Bird' Parker, helped bebop spread outside of Harlem, New York (DeVeaux, 1997, pp. 364–6).

By the late 1940s, there was an interest in bebop in the Netherlands (van de Leur, 2018, pp. 181–2), and several jazz fans formed their own clubs to listen to and discuss modern jazz records together, as well as organise concerts and jam sessions (van de Leur, 2018, p. 182). Logan performed at these sessions with his five-piece Freddy's Small Combo (Fats, 1949), or by sitting in with others at clubs like the Jig Rhythm Club (Swank, 1949). In the meantime, Dutch singer and pianist Pia Beck had left jazz sextet The Millers to form her own group and asked Logan to join her trio in November 1949, with Carel de Vogel on guitar as their third member (Leerink, 1950).

The Pia Beck Trio began with a residency at the Cockpit in the busy thoroughfare of Leidsestraat before being invited to perform in theatres across England and Scotland in 1950 (Beck, 1982, p. 33). The tour was a success and they returned later that year for further engagements in England. These included performances on the same programme as the Black American jazz singer Nellie Lutcher (Beck, 1982, p. 34) and English groups such as Kenny Graham and his Afro-Cubists (Pitt, 1950).

Across the Netherlands, opinions continued to rage around jazz and its many forms, including debates over modern jazz. Some of these arguments appeared in the Dutch magazine *The 45 Club News* (Kleinhout, 2006, p. 139), where an article comparing New Orleans jazz and bebop appeared in late 1950 by Michiel de Ruyter. This provoked a response from Freddy Logan, who challenged some of de Ruyter's statements (Kleinhout, 2006, p. 183). Logan wrote, 'New Orleans Jazz is at a standstill and bop, or "New Jazz", is being developed further and further, the latter against all predictions.' To make his argument, Logan listed the Tadd Dameron's Orchestra, and Miles Davis's 'Move' and 'Godchild' as examples de Ruyter should hear to better understand his point (Loggen, 1951).

The two Davis singles were released between 1949 and 1950 (Pollard, 1950) and later collected on Davis's landmark album *Birth of the Cool* in 1957 (Welding, 1989). Of those, 'Move' would have continued importance for Logan, who recorded his own rendition ten years later for The Three Out.

Back in 1950, Logan made his first studio recordings with the Pia Beck Trio in September, recording 'Pia's Boogie' (Lord, 1992, p. B345), which became a great success for Beck (Twentsch Dagblad Tubantia, 1952). Following a second session in June 1951 (Lord, 1992, p. B345), Logan left the group that September (Openneer, 1996) and joined the Guus Van Manen Trio. This trio was praised by *Philharmonic* magazine for their modern sound, noting listeners seeking 'interesting tones, intelligent phrasing, but above all spontaneous, fascinating, modern music' would find satisfaction from their music (Sam, 1952). The group toured Germany (Rhythme, 1953a) and recorded two songs as the Guus Van Manen Kwartet (Van Eyle, 1981, p. 145). Logan then returned to Germany with his own group, The Fred Loggen Quintet, who were hailed by *Rhythme* as a 'Dutch all-star combo' of 'ultramodern soloists' (Rhythme, 1953b) and by *Philharmonic*, which wrote they were a new group that the Netherlands could be proud of (hrd, 1953).

Before leaving the Netherlands, Logan had met the Australian actress and model Lucille Power. Originally from Bellevue, New South Wales (Rolfe, 1954), Power left Australia in May 1952 (The Mirror, 1952) and travelled to the Netherlands to work as a model. There, she met Logan (Rolfe, 1954). The two were married in October 1953 in Amsterdam (De Telegraaf, 1953) and Lucille Power joined Logan's group as their vocalist.

After several months of touring through Western Europe, Logan decided to disband the group in December 1953 and settle in London with his wife (Music Maker, 1956). It was here that he took his first professional bass lessons (Anon., 1958), studying at the Guildhall School of Music in London (Dutch Australian Weekly, 1956). During this time, he integrated himself into the English jazz scene (Music Maker, 1956).

Jazz had been in England for much the same length of time as in the Netherlands and was particularly popular in London (Harris, 1957, p. 219). After bebop was introduced to England in 1945 (Kinsella, 2022, pp. vii, 75), the jazz scene split between the traditional New Orleans style and modern bebop forms (Godbolt, 1984, pp. 268–9). The modern scene was small and primarily focused around jazz clubs in London's Soho area (Kinsella, 2022, pp. 71, 90), including The Flamingo (Solly, 2012).

Kenny Graham's Afro-Cubists were The Flamingo's resident band when it opened in 1952 (Solly, 2012), and soon after Freddy Logan arrived in England in 1954, he took part in two recording sessions with Graham, released over four shellac 10″ discs by Esquire (Lord, 1994a, p. G487). The group had formed in 1950 to merge modern jazz with African percussion and Cuban rhythms (Whitcomb, 1950). These included congas and maracas on *Jeepers Creepers*, alongside Graham on alto saxophone, Dave Goldberg on guitar and Logan's bass (Alaronde, 1955).

Following the Afro-Cuban jazz of Kenny Graham, Logan joined modern jazz pianist Derek Smith's trio to record the second and third volumes in a series titled *Jazz at the Flamingo* (Lord, 1994b, p. J209) before recording with another regular of The Flamingo, tenor saxophonist Tommy Whittle (Lord, 2001, p. W599). These would be collected on Whittle's album

Spotlighting, released in June 1956, with the album sleeve notes introducing Logan:

> Freddie Logan, from Holland, plays five string bass, is a [American jazz bassist Jimmy] Blanton fan, with a fast effortless-seeming technique. His good tone, says Esquire chief Carlo Krahmer, is especially easy to record.

> (Whittle, 1956)

Alongside his recording work, by the mid-1950s Freddy Logan was playing across five different jazz clubs in England with saxophonists Johnny Dankworth, Ronnie Scott, Joe Temperley, Tubby Hayes, trumpeter Jimmy Deuchar and trombonist Keith Christie. Additionally, he was also touring with his own trio (Music Maker, 1956). Following his studies, Logan played with the US Air Force, which took him to North Africa (European Stars And Stripes, 1954, p. 43), before he and his wife travelled to Australia, departing 26 June 1956 on board the S.S. *Orontes* from England to Sydney with their two-month-old son John F. Loggen (Ancestry, 1956, pp. 1, 23). Originally their plan had been to make a short visit to see family before travelling on to America, but Logan liked Australia so they settled in Sydney and he became involved in the local jazz scene (Dutch Australian Weekly, 1956).

Mike Nock: Jazz in New Zealand

Michael Anthony Nock was born 27 September 1940 in Christchurch, New Zealand. His family left Christchurch when he was young and settled in the small-town of Ngaruawahia on New Zealand's North Island. Here Nock's father began teaching him piano when he was eleven years old. Soon after, Nock made his first public performance and formed a band with others from his neighbourhood inspired by the humorous jazz records of Spike Jonse and his City Slickers. Nock composed some of his first songs for the group to play (Meehan, 2010, pp. 17–19).

Jazz had been heard across New Zealand since the early 1920s, initially through live performances from touring musicians, gramophone records (Bourke, 2013, pp. 64–5) and radio broadcasts (Ward, 2012, p. 56). By the mid-1940s, the new modern style of bebop had arrived thanks to American records and radio broadcasts (Ward, 2012, p. 226). Unlike how it was perceived overseas, where schisms had formed between fans of traditional and modern jazz, bebop was more warmly embraced in New Zealand, perhaps due to an overall smaller jazz scene (Ward, 2012, p. 228). Jazz could be heard on *Rhythm on Record*, a radio programme hosted by Arthur Peace since the late 1930s, where he often played jazz records and included live performances from jazz bands (Bollinger, 2020). Mike Nock was a regular listener, as he explained:

> In those days, pop and jazz were all mixed up together, because there wasn't the division that there is now. And the one thing that spearheaded my interest in jazz, was Arthur Pearce who had a radio show on Friday night. He'd play the latest stuff from the US, Dixieland to avantgarde, and people used to listen to this stuff and get together to talk about it, fostering this conversation, and that really got a hold on me. I didn't know anything about jazz. I knew the music I liked, and my favourite was an American piano player called Charlie Kunz. He played standard tunes, but they were always playing him on the radio, and if you hear something enough it has an effect. There was also Winifred Atwell, and one of the very first pieces that I ever played in public was Winifred Atwell's 'Black and White Rag'. I played it in concert when I was 12.
>
> (Nock, 2024)

Winifred Atwell was a Black English pianist, born in Trinidad. She toured Australia and New Zealand in 1955 (Newcastle Morning Herald and Miners' Advocate, 1954) where her playing style was described as 'hot, fast and loud' (Nicholas, 1954). Atwell's preference was to perform on an old detuned honky tonk piano which gave a distinctive sound that was popular with audiences (Tomes, 2024, pp. 192–3). The success of songs like Atwell's 'Black and White Rag' came during a revival of the honky tonk and ragtime styles during the 1940s and 1950s (Gammond, 1976, pp. 173–4). Outside of England, she had significant success in Australia where she relocated permanently during the 1970s (Tomes, 2024, pp. 191, 193).

While Atwell had been an early hero of Nock's, this would change when he heard Bud Powell by chance one evening (Clare & Brennan, 1995, p. 68). Nock was listening to the radio again when they played music from *Jazz at Massey Hall* (Meehan, 2010, p. 20), an album featuring trumpeter Dizzy Gillespie, saxophonist Charlie Parker, bassist Charles Mingus, drummer Max Roach and pianist Bud Powell, recorded and released in 1953 (Hentoff, 1953). Nock recalled:

> I thought, this is the greatest thing I'd ever heard. Turns out they were one of the seminal bands in bebop, world famous, even at the time, and I didn't even know. I thought it was a New Zealand band. I thought, I want to play like that, so I started playing like that.
>
> (Bhatt, 2024)

Nock's father had been teaching him the ragtime style on piano until his sudden death, an event that saw the young Mike Nock channel his anger into an obsession with music (Meehan, 2010, p. 20). He received further piano lessons from local pharmacist and pianist Bert McNamara, who lent Nock records by American musicians Art Tatum, George Shearing and Nat 'King' Cole, for him to learn by ear. When Cole toured New Zealand in 1955, Nock made the trip to Auckland to see him perform, later saying the music blew his mind (Meehan, 2010, pp. 21–2).

Soon after, the Nock family moved again – this time to the small city of Nelson on the South Island of New Zealand. There, Nock no longer had a music teacher and instead relied on books to teach himself how to read music and also to play both the piano and alto saxophone. Although he eventually met other jazz fans and joined a local jazz club (Meehan, 2010, p. 25), Nock wanted more than the small city could offer. In 1956 he left home for Wellington, New Zealand's capital (Meehan, 2010, p. 27).

After sometime working with bands as a pianist and saxophonist, Nock joined a group called The Fabulous Flamingos, who immediately pawned his saxophone for money, forcing Nock to abandon that instrument entirely (Lewis & Lewis, 1992, p. 13). By 1957, Nock had left the Flamingos and moved to Auckland (Meehan, 2010, pp. 31–2), where he began making uncredited appearances on recordings such as Johnny Cooper's 'Pie Cart Rock 'n' Roll' (Various, 2003). Recorded in 1957, the song was considered New Zealand's first rock and roll song, with Cooper dubbed the country's 'King of rock and roll' (Carlyon, 2013). Cooper then discovered and mentored Johnny Devlin in early 1957 (Thompson, 2002). Devlin would become New Zealand's first rock and roll star. Nock joined Devlin on some of his early recordings after meeting Devlin's manager Phil Warren at a local jazz club (Meehan, 2010, p. 32). Four songs recorded in June 1958 were released on Warren's Prestige label as an EP titled *How Would 'Ya Be* (Devlin, 1958). Nock then recorded another rock and roll EP in December with an uncredited appearance on the Bob Paris Combo's self-titled debut as well as an uncredited appearance with The Auckland Jive Centre Band (Grigg, n.d.).

Considered one of Auckland's top jazz musicians at the time, Nock wanted more and set his sights on the United States, where all of his favourite musicians came from (Meehan, 2010, p. 36). To get there, Nock felt his best route was via Australia, so he stowed away on a boat, hiding in a friend's cabin. He arrived in Sydney in 1958, aged eighteen (Nock, 2024).

Upon his arrival, Nock made friends fast and worked as a pianist in various groups over the next few years, including with Australian rock and roll star Johnny O'Keefe (Reid, 2024). As he later explained:

> Some of the first people I met in Australia were jazz musicians like Bob Bertles, Bernie McGann and John Pochée, and they're the ones who got me into O'Keefe's band. But for a jazz player, those rock 'n' roll songs were all pretty basic three-chord stuff and it wasn't very challenging for me.
>
> (*The Canberra Times*, 2006)

Nock found the work too similar to what he'd been working on in Auckland with Johnny Devlin, having thought that he was leaving rock behind to focus on jazz (Sharpe, 2008, p. 313). But it did allow him to work with talented jazz musicians such as Bob Bertles, and get paid for it. He recalled:

> It was good money, a bit of fun, and it was great that Bob was on the gig, but I wasn't interested in the music. Later when rock and roll developed I began to find it more interesting. But that early period of rock and roll was pretty boring for a piano player … It had no connection to anything we did in the jazz world. The rock scene was a totally foreign world

to what I was interested in … At one stage Johnny O'Keefe wanted to write some songs with me and I wasn't at all interested. I was just too blinkered.

(Sharpe, 2008, p. 313)

In Sydney, Nock was making a name for himself as one of the city's best young pianists (Nettelbeck, 2020, p. 5) and was performing at the El Rocco jazz club with a group including Colin Jones on trumpet, Gerry Gardiner on bass, Bob Bertles on alto and Stewart Speer on drums. They played 'hard bop' in the style of American bandleader Art Blakey (Jones, 2024).

In April 1959, Nock joined saxophonist Frank Thornton's group in Coolangatta, Queensland, where saxophonist Bob Gillett was also part of the band (Hall, 1959). Nock said the two musicians took him under their wings, and he performed with them both again separately in the coming years (Nock, 2024). Thornton then left for Melbourne, where he would be leading a band in a new restaurant. When he later needed a pianist, Nock was invited to join. It was in Melbourne that Nock began working with drummer Chris Karan (Nock, 2022).

Chris Karan: Jazz in Australia

Chrisostomos Karanikis was born on 14 October 1939 to Greek parents in Carlton, an inner-city suburb of Melbourne, Australia. Soon after he was born his family moved to nearby West Brunswick, where he grew up (Karan, 2022a). At home, Chris Karan, as he would be better known, heard a lot of Greek and Turkish music played, while his older brother Peter introduced him to jazz and Cuban music (Vulture, 2006). 'He used to bring home a few 78's every Friday which ended up becoming an enormous and varied collection so there was always something new to listen to', Karan said (Vulture, 2006).

At the time, Australia had a large number of jazz fans who were collecting records (Bell, 1988, p. 59), members of clubs or musicians in their own right, with jazz having had several peaks in popularity around the country since the 1920s (Johnson, 1987, pp. 3, 17, 47). When Columbia Graphophone Company opened their record pressing plant in Sydney in 1926, it was considered to be the beginning of the record industry in Australia as they began producing shellac 78 RPM discs (The National Film and Sound Archive of Australia, 2014), including several jazz discs by overseas artists (Discogs, 2025a).

Many Australians had first heard jazz while stationed overseas during the First World War where American jazz bands performed for troops, inspiring Australian jazz bands to form following the war (Bisset, 1987, pp. 12, 14–17). Local recordings from this era featured a style mixing the sounds of American jazz, English dance bands and Australia's theatre pit orchestras (Bisset, 1987, p. 30). Keen musicians were pleased to be able to perform with the Americans when they toured Australia (Bisset, 1987, p. 23). But, for the majority of Australian jazz fans, there was little chance to see Black American musicians perform locally over the coming decades.

This was because the Australian government had adopted the *Immigration Restriction Act of 1901*, better known as the White Australia policy. It saw the government adopt discriminatory measures to exclude non-white immigrants and keep Australia 'British' (National Archives of Australia, n.d.). This policy was adopted by the Musicians' Union of Australia under the guise of protecting the jobs of Australian musicians. There were exceptions, however, such as a tour by Black American Sonny Clay and his band Sonny Clay's Colored

Idea in 1928 (Bisset, 1987, p. 44). They were granted visas after the Tivoli Theatre management sidestepped the Musicians' Union by listing Clay and his band as theatrical artists rather than musicians (O'Connell, 2021, pp. 84–5).

Nevertheless, Clay encountered trouble with local authorities and unions who were incensed that a Black band was performing to such success. They were ultimately deported (Bisset, 1987, pp. 44–6). The Musicians' Union of Australia then enforced their existing 'no colored [*sic*]' rule banning Black musicians from visiting Australia. This lasted until the mid-1950s (O'Connell, 2021, pp. 62, 249).

Despite the ban, jazz grew locally. During the 1930s, Jim Davidson's Dance Band performed their swing style of jazz nationally on ABC Radio. This was then released on record by Columbia Records (Rippin, 1948). The Second World War again allowed some musicians stationed overseas to play with Americans, while Americans stationed in Australia meant their jazz bands came too, giving some local musicians another chance to hear jazz played by the Americans (Bisset, 1987, pp. 76–7). Young Australians were also being employed to keep the Americans entertained, with singer Les Welch forming a band with reeds player Don Burrows and trumpeter Ron Falson, both teenagers at the time (Bisset, 1987, p. 80). They would make their own impact on Australian jazz in later years (Johnson, 1987, pp. 123–4, 153). Burrows also appeared at the Booker T. Washington club in Sydney, a private club for Black American servicemen, with the band made up of white Australian musicians (Bisset, 1987, pp. 83–5).

Following the war, in 1946 Ampersand records was founded by Bill Miller as the first specialist label dedicated to Australian jazz (Victorian Jazz Archive, 2013). Other small local record labels began to release Australian jazz too, while larger commercial labels released jazz from the United States and UK. Thanks to these efforts, locally recorded jazz became more widely heard and Australians kept up to date with the latest sounds (Rippin, 1948). ABC radio aired bebop for the first time in 1946 by playing discs such as Dizzy Gillespie's 'Salt Peanuts' (Whiteoak, 1985, pp. 76, 97). The Gillespie discs were said to inspire greater interest in modern jazz at the time and further experimentation among local musicians as they were introduced to the new sound (Whiteoak, 1985, p. 97).

At the same time, traditional Dixieland jazz remained popular. The annual Australian Jazz Convention was first held in 1946 and gathered jazz performers from across Australia (Bisset, 1987, p. 114). Modern jazz styles were banned, with the Convention intended to 'further the original Dixieland style of playing' (The Sun-Herald, 1950). This restriction was only somewhat eased during the 1970s (Bisset, 1987, p. 131).

Don Banks recorded what has been claimed to be the 'first Australian bop composition' in 1947, 'Feeling Dizzy' (Whiteoak, 1985, p. 83). It blended his group's own style of jazz with elements of bebop to create their own take on modern jazz (Whiteoak, 1985, p. 90). However, it was only available on private acetate (Kennedy, 2015). Banks's group included Errol Buddle on reeds, who next contributed to 'Buddles Be-Bop Boogie', recorded by the Jack Brokensha Quartet in 1948 and released on the Jazz Art label (Kennedy, 2015). This new label had been set up with the purpose of releasing Australian modern jazz (Whiteoak, 1985, p. 99). Their recordings show examples of how the musicians incorporated their own ideas and experiments in modern jazz as it continued to develop within Australia (Whiteoak, 1985, p. 113). At the same time, the general public were introduced to modern jazz through a series of battles of the bands featuring a traditional jazz group and a modern bebop group. Audiences could then vote on which they preferred. For example, when traditionalists The Port Jackson Jazz Band went up against beboppers Ron Falson's Harbour City Six in one battle, the traditionalist won (Whiteoak, 1985, pp. 99–101).

Unfortunately for jazz fans, Australia began restricting many imported products in 1952, including gramophone records (The Argus, 1952). This led to limited stock available in record stores (S.S., 1952a), with many records made impossible to purchase at all (S.S., 1952b). Graeme Bell, considered one of Australia's best known jazz musicians at the time (Rippin, 1949, pp. 27–9), was critical of the move. He saw it as an act to further isolate Australia as it supplemented the ban on foreign musicians touring Australia (Bell, 1952):

> For Australia to be geographically situated so far from other countries is bad enough, but to have a Musicians' Union which will not allow overseas bands to visit us is a bit hard to take. I was never prevented from taking my band into any country in Europe. And now, the final touches have been put to our citadel of isolation by the import restrictions on overseas recordings.
>
> (Bell, 1952)

The import restrictions were introduced at the same time as the introduction of new microgroove technology that saw record labels move away from 78 RPM speed to 45 and 33 1/3 RPM. This new technology allowed more music to be included on each disc. By the end of 1952, Australian pressing plants were manufacturing their own microgroove LPs (S.S., 1952c) and as import restrictions eased there was a greater mix of records available to Australians again (S.S., 1954). This enabled young fans like Chris Karan to hear the latest jazz at home, as he continued listening to his brother's growing record collection (Karan, 2025).

Karan began learning drums at school when he was around twelve years old, and incorporated a wide range of influences he heard on records into his own playing. These included the 'real Latin kick' heard on albums by the George Shearing Quintet, the Indian classical tabla playing of Alla Rakha and the jazz percussion of Gene Krupa, among others (Vulture, 2006):

> I was listening mainly to the West Coast music from the very beginning. Like Shirley Rodgers, Shirley Mann, Earl Bud Powell, and Bud Shank. Then I started listening to Art Blackey, Horace Silver, John Coltrane, and I moved over to the East Coast. That was the kind of music I was really interested in. That and the Blue Note label.
>
> (Karan, 2025)

Karan left school to become an apprentice cabinet maker when he was sixteen. However, after six months he decided he wanted to pursue being a musician instead:

> I got fed up, and I wanted to play professionally. My first job came up with Sergio Fochi. It was guitar, accordion, bass, and drums, at The Oriental Hotel on Collins Street, and I was working six nights a week.
>
> (Karan, 2025)

He also found time to sit in at local jazz clubs, including Jazz Centre 44 (Karan, 2025). This club was started by Horst Liepolt in 1957. Liepolt had arrived in Australia from Germany in 1951 and opened Jazz Centre 44 in St Kilda. It has been called 'the first modern jazz club in Australia', though one night each week audiences could also hear traditional jazz when the Melbourne New Orleans Jazz Band appeared (Blum, 2019). Among the club's modern groups were The Brian Brown Quintet, 'the top modern outfit in Melbourne', according to Liepolt (Blum, 2018). They performed a mix of their own compositions and those by Americans like trumpeter Miles Davis, trombonist J. J. Johnson and saxophonist Sonny Rollins (Brian Brown Quintet, 1977). Another band, led by vibraphonist Allan Lee featured Chris Karan:

> It was quite an interesting venue to the young jazz players at that time, and another place called The South Pacific which was right on the beach, where I'd go and sit in occasionally too.
>
> (Karan, 2022b)

Karan kept busy then, and sitting in with bands around Melbourne and performing with Sergio Fochi's band at the Oriental Hotel six nights each week.

After the Oriental Hotel, Karan moved to The Tarantella, a nightclub in St Kilda where he played with Wolf Abramowitz's Orchestra. This also included Sergio Fochi (Karan, 2025). In 1958, Abramowitz took the band north to The Flamingo Restaurant in Surfers Paradise (Wolf Abramowitz, 1958), a suburb of the Gold Coast, Queensland. While there, Karan met American saxophonist Frank Thornton, who was putting together a new band for a club in Melbourne, as Karan later recalled:

> I did a season up in Surfers Paradise, and I used to visit the Surfers Paradise Hotel, which had a small band there. I used to sit in and the saxophone player was Frank Thornton who said, 'I'm actually going down to Melbourne, and then this new club is opening. If it comes off, would you like me to give you a call? And would you like to join the group?' I said 'Yeah, I'd love to'. He said that there's also some American

guests that are coming, as well, and it's going to be a very sprauncy place in Toorak Road called The Embers. So, that was that. I ended up going back down to Melbourne and then I got a call. It really happened.

(Karan, 2022a)

Thornton had impressed several people with his tenor saxophone as he played hotels across Queensland's Gold Coast that year. Among them was Mike Nock, who had joined Thornton's band in April 1959 (Hall, 1959). But although Nock and Chris Karan both performed with Thornton around the same time, they wouldn't meet one another until they were both in Melbourne (Karan, 2022b).

2 Jazz in Melbourne and Sydney

The Embers

The Embers was located on Toorak Rd, South Yarra, Melbourne. Nearly 400 people attended the opening on 3 August 1959 (The Age, 1959a). The Frank Thornton Quintette were the house band. This included Australians Chris Karan and saxophonist Frank Smith, with Black Americans, pianist Wilmus Reeves, bassist Carl Brown and singer Barbara Virgil (The Embers, 1959).

Frank Smith had been active in the Australian jazz scene since the 1940s as a reeds player (Johnson, 1987, p. 254). He had a strong reputation that led Mike Nock to call him 'the best saxophonist in the country' (Nettelbeck, 2017). He appeared on the 1957 Music Maker All Star album (Nettelbeck, 2017) but otherwise recorded little (Johnson, 1987, p. 255). Barbara Virgil had grown up in California, then moved to New York and made a name for herself on the cabaret scene before she was booked to appear in Australia (The Sacramento Bee, 1959). Both Wilmus Reeves and Carl Brown had played with several leading jazz musicians in America including trombonist J. J. Johnson and saxophonists Charlie Parker and Stan Getz (Powerhouse, 1959). In Melbourne, Reeves and Brown lived together. Chris Karan recalled that whenever he visited, they would be listening to Charlie Parker records: 'Byrd would be playing on the turntable, [because] Carl was a maniac for Charlie Parker. He loved his playing, like we all do' (Karan, 2022a).

The Frank Thornton Quintette broadcast live from The Embers one month after the club opened (The Age, 1959b). Then owner Jimmy Knowles organized an album session which was recorded over three days in the restaurant (Karan, 2022b). Chris Karan recalled:

> That was a great idea. I'd never cut an album with anybody at that time, because I was still quite young and hadn't met the right people. The whole group sounded pretty nice, and definitely had to be recorded, so Jimmy organised it. It was all live, and we didn't repeat anything. We just played our usual arrangements and tunes we did most nights, they recorded everything, and then chose the pieces that were going to be part of the album. We listened to a lot of the takes from different days, and I think they chose most of the best ones.
>
> (Karan, 2022b)

The album *Jazz At The Embers* was released in May 1960 and featured The Frank Thornton Quintette and Barbara Virgil credited as The Embers Quintet (De Looper, 2025a, p. 75). In their review *Music Maker* praised the spontaneity of the live recording, and felt it was as good as anything else being produced around the world, though they seemed disappointed that only two Australians were featured in the lineup (Music Maker, 1960b). *The Sun-Herald* wrote the band 'swings mightily with a happy anarchy', with Wilmus Reeves's piano dominating the album (Downbeat, 1960a). However, before the album had been released, there were several changes at The Embers.

Reeves and Brown left before the end of 1959 as they felt the music they were required to play was too commercial. Billy Weston, a trombonist from Sydney, was called in to join the band and he invited Mike Nock who replaced Reeves, along with bassist Pete Robinson, who replaced Brown (Meehan, 2010, p. 39). Weston was only briefly with the band (National Library of Australia, n.d.), but Robinson and Nock stayed on, much to the pleasure of Karan as the two had previously met before playing together at The Embers, though neither recalls now where it was exactly. Karan explained:

> There were two things at the age of 18 and 19 that were really nice and very rewarding. One was meeting up with Frank and joining The Embers band. And the other one was meeting up with Mike, who I really loved being with. He was such a lovely guy, a terrific player, and very rewarding as well. And of course, then he actually joined the group in The Embers, because the band broke up and Mike came in.
>
> (Karan, 2022a)

While Nock had been happy to take the job, he didn't play there long because on 9 November 1959 the building caught fire. Hundreds of patrons ran for cover, though Nock and Karan were a bit slow to realise what was happening. Nock remembers:

> We were experimenting with dope at the time, and were both a bit high. Then we realised we had better get out of there. I had all this music that was all gone. People screaming. Guys pushing their dates out of the window, and we just strolled out all cool. The club was pretty fancy, and after it burnt down, they put up a big sign saying The Ashes.
>
> (Nock, 2024)

Ironically, the fire began moments after it was announced that Barbara Virgil would sing 'Fire Down Below'.

The band played on until everyone had safely left the building (The Age, 1959c). However, all of their instruments were lost in the fire. Karan recalled:

> We lost this lovely grand piano and my drum kit and everything else. I tried to rush back to save my cymbals and the firemen grabbed me by the neck. I said, 'I need to get my cymbals' and he said, 'You're not going in there,' and he pushed me over. That was the end of it.
>
> (Karan, 2022a)

The band were paid over the summer on the condition that they didn't play anywhere else, so they spent the time rehearsing (Karan, 2022a). During their downtime, Frank Smith worked with Mike Nock on his playing and Nock later highlighted Smith as one of the teachers who left a significant influence on his work (Meehan, 2010, p. 41).

When The Embers reopened in February 1960, owner Jimmy Knowles told the band they should play more commercial music and wear chef hats, similar to the restaurant logo, to the disgust of Nock. 'That didn't go down well at all. I was a very feisty young kid, and he didn't tell me what to do, not that shit! So, we came to words, I refused to do that, and came to Sydney' (Nock, 2024). Karan soon followed as he explained:

> When Mike left The Embers, I decided to leave as well. Because he was going back to Sydney and I thought, well I wouldn't mind going up there as well, so I did. I didn't do anything for a little while and hung around. Then I heard about this night club in the city, called Sammy Lee's Latin Quarter. I decided to go down with a couple of friends and I saw this conga drum there, and I said, 'Do you mind if I sit in?' and I did. Then the boss of Sammy's said they had a

cabaret coming and asked if I'd like to be part of it because they needed a conga drummer. So, I did a couple of weeks cabaret in a nightclub, which was not the type of thing I thought I'd be doing. But it was a start.

(Karan, 2025)

Soon after, Karan signed a six-month contract to play at the Rex Hotel on Macleay Street, Kings Cross, with accordionist Ronnie Fabri (Karan, 2025). Rex Hotels were a chain spread around Sydney (The Sydney Morning Herald, 1960a), each featuring their own bands. Freddy Logan had played at the Rex in Bondi with vibraphonist Pat Caplice (Dutch Australian Weekly, 1956) but the Rex in Kings Cross was the most well-known as it hosted international celebrities such as Frank Sinatra during his Sydney stay (Roberts, 2014). While Chris Karan was engaged at the Rex, Mike Nock played any gig he could get until he caught the eye of Freddy Logan (Meehan, 2010, pp. 42–3).

Jazz Club 11 and El Rocco

While Nock and Karan had been at The Embers in Melbourne, Freddy Logan had been integrating himself into the Sydney jazz scene. Shortly after arriving in Australia, Logan formed Jazz Club 11 with drummer Don Osborne. The club had its opening night on 13 January 1957 at the New Sheridan, Oxford Street, Woollahra (Brown, 1957). The New Sheridan was a converted ballroom with a large dance floor and bar owned by infamous Sydney nightclub figure Sammy Lee (Trueman, 2025). It could fit 350 seated patrons (Trueman, 2025). Jazz Club 11 regularly attracted between 250 and 300 enthusiastic jazz fans (Music Maker, 1957a).

Logan told *Music Maker* magazine he wanted to emulate the jazz clubs in England and allow younger musicians to sit in with those more experienced to create a higher standard of jazz in Australia (Music Maker, 1957b). A separate Sydney Jazz Club had already been active for a number of years (Johnson, 1983b) but was focused on 'Traditional Dixieland Jazz Music' (Sydney Jazz Club, 1957), while Jazz Club 11 featured modern jazz (Music Maker, 1957b).

Alongside its founders, Jazz Club 11 included bands made up of reeds players Don Burrows and Dave Ruteledge, trumpeter Ron Falson, drummer Cyril Bevan and guitarist Jan Gold (Music Maker, 1957c). Drummer and vibraphonist Pat Caplice was among those who visited the club and played there. He was extremely impressed by Logan's drive to raise the standard of Australian jazz, as he explained:

> Freddy was a young, interesting jazz man, and he got onto me because I was, with a couple of others like Don Burrows, wanting to raise the bar and stop just fiddling around with 84 bars of the blues. He was the only young guy who was boosting the talent that was available, and giving people a chance to hear [something] that wasn't all just playing the blues. Guys like Freddy started it happening.
>
> (Caplice, 2022)

Those who played at Jazz Club 11 were considered some of the best jazz musicians in Australia at the time, a fact cemented when magazine *Music Maker* opened their 1957 Australian Musician's Poll, calling on readers to vote for their favourite Australian jazz musicians and vocalists (Music Maker, 1957d). Among the poll winners were several regulars of Jazz Club 11. Freddy Logan won in the bass category, and the Jazz Club 11 Octet lost in the Small Group category to the Pat Caplice Trio by only two votes (Music Maker, 1957e). A representative group from the winners were selected to record an album as part of Parlophone's *Jazz in Australia* series (Music Maker, 1957f).

Beginning in 1955, the series had focused on Dixieland jazz acts such as by Paramount Jazz Band, and Graeme Bell, rather than those playing in the newer modern style (Discogs, 2025b). Because of this, the series had been criticised for sounding like 'museum relics' featuring 'young men playing old men's music' and led *The Sun-Herald*'s Downbeat column to ask, 'Can there be an Australian jazz?' (Downbeat, 1957a). At the time they felt Australian jazz records sounded as though Australia existed in isolation of any new ideas in jazz. There were, though, a few exceptions. Pat Caplice was highlighted as the only musician brave enough to add bold modernism to his work and Don Burrows was also noted to have tentatively ventured into modern stylings in his own (Downbeat, 1957a). Both Caplice and Burrows were among the Music Maker poll winners who took part in the 1957 recording session in which *Music Maker* said they wanted to show the best aspects of Australian jazz, allowing the musicians a rare opportunity to play the style of music they liked without worrying about whether it would be commercial (Music Maker, 1957g).

Four songs were recorded over two days in July that year, and Freddy Logan appeared on each one (Music Maker, 1957f). The 10" album *Jazz in Australia Volume 5* was released 26 September 1957 credited to The 'Music Maker' 1957 All Stars (Music Maker, 1957g). Downbeat reviewed the album one month after their column criticizing Australian jazz and wrote it was like a 'breath of fresh air' compared to other Australian jazz records. They liked the album's modern sound, and called it 'the key of the door for Australian jazz' which needed to be heard (Downbeat, 1957b).

Following the All Stars album, Logan continued to take part in other sessions and joined Graeme Bell & His Skiffle Gang for some studio recordings in late 1957 (Lord, 1992, p. B375). Their single 'Freight Train' was released by Columbia in August that year and became a Top 10 hit, selling seven thousand copies in one week, and was voted the best Australian disc of the year (Bell, 1988, pp. 251, 253).

Members of the Music Maker All Stars continued to appear together regularly, and reunited as Freddy Logan's All Stars in 1958 when Logan hosted his own radio programme *Jazz For Pleasure*. The programme featured Dave Rutledge (tenor and alto sax, and flute), Don Burrows (clarinet), Ron Webber (drums) and Terry Wilkinson (piano) (Music Maker, 1958a), who Logan felt compared favourably with the leading jazz musicians from America and Europe (Victor Harbour Times, 1958).

Jazz for Pleasure drew a big following as each Wednesday they'd improvise around songs submitted by their listeners in what they termed 'lugging' (Music Maker, 1958b). They then gained a residency at the newly opened Sky Lounge on Pitt Street, Sydney (Music Maker, 1958c), where they took the name The Australian All-Stars (All-Stars, 1960). This began as a promotion between Jazz Club 11 and Sky Lounge owner Graeme Bennett's Australian Jazz Club (Music Maker, 1958c), before Jazz Club 11 officially merged into Bennett's club (All-Stars, 1960). The band played jazz standards each Sunday (Music Maker, 1958c) such as Cole Porter's 'Love for Sale' (Nettelbeck, 2020, p. 4). Terry Wilkinson later described the Sky Lounge and their audience:

> It was a place for dancing jitterbug type dancing. The kids were looking for something to do on a Sunday. Some had their rock venues where there would be people like Normie

Rowe and Johnny O'Keefe, but the Sky Lounge was a place
where twenty year olds could jitterbug to jazz instead, if they
didn't dig O'Keefe type music. It was a good place and we
played good music.

(Sharpe, 2008, p. 34)

Between 500 and 700 people came to see the All-Stars each week (Music Maker, 1960a). They recorded two albums, *Jazz for Beach-Niks* and *Jazz for Beach-Niks Volume 2*, both released in 1960 (Downbeat, 1960b). In 1959 the All-Stars also began appearing on TV (Sterne, 1959).

Six O'Clock Rock, a television programme targeted at Australian teenagers broadcast by the ABC, first aired on Saturday 28 February 1959 (Starlite International, 1989). It featured a mix of rock from Johnny O'Keefe and jazz from The Australian All-Stars (Giuffre, 2016, p. 123). After several appearances, The Australian All-Stars were given their own self-titled live programme featuring the band performing for thirty minutes alongside guest vocalists (The Sydney Morning Herald, 1959a). They still appeared on *Six O'Clock Rock*. However, by August, The Australian All-Stars were dropped from the programme as the cost of employing two bands was considered too much for the ABC (Giuffre, 2016, p. 124) and the jazz component of *Six O'Clock Rock* was largely forgotten (Giuffre, 2016, p. 117). That same month, their own self-titled programme was merged with another variety show *Make Ours Music*, where they performed seven modern jazz songs in the extended sixty-minute format (The Sydney Morning Herald, 1959b). They continued to be part of this programme until at least the end of October 1959 (The Age, 1959d).

With the success of the All-Stars, Freddy Logan remained in demand as a bass player. During this period, he recorded with the English pianist Joe Loufer (Music Maker, 1958d), The Don Burrows Six (Music Maker, 1958e), visiting US singer Russ Arno (Downbeat, 1959) and with his own group The Loganberries, who released two singles of their own (De Looper, 2025a, p. 21). But Logan would soon put all his focus into a new group after meeting Mike Nock, who by early 1960 was in Sydney again recording with his own band.

The Mike Nock Orchestra featured Nock with saxophonist Ray Swinburne, guitarist Neville Chamberlain, bassist Ron Martin and drummers Colin Bailey and Cyril Bevan (Mitchell, 1988, p. 170). They recorded with pop singers The Powell Twins, American sisters who had previously released two singles in the 1950s (Global Recording Artists, n.d.) and were flown to Australia to appear on television. Their recordings with Nock were released on two 7" records in 1961 (National Film and Sound Archive of Australia, 1998) but before then Nock had returned to playing at the El Rocco (Johnson, 1983a).

The El Rocco Jazz Cellar was a small downstairs restaurant on King Street, Sydney managed by Arthur James that had opened in 1955 as a coffee shop (Clare & Brennan, 1995, pp. 59–60). It would be considered full with only sixty people inside (The Sydney Morning Herald, 1959c). The restaurant's initial claim to fame was that they had a TV installed in 1957 (Clare & Brennan, 1995, p. 59).

Television in Australia was still a novelty. Black-and-white broadcasts had only begun in late 1956 (The Sydney Morning Herald, 1956a) and included a mixture of Australian and American programmes (The Sydney Morning Herald, 1956b). Early Australian programmes such as *Look Who's Dropped In* featured performances by Australian jazz musicians including bandleader Graeme Bell (ABC Weekly, 1957), who also hosted his own programme (The Sydney Morning Herald, 1956c).

American variety programmes such as *The Steve Allen Show* were popular as they also sometimes featured jazz musicians (Clare & Brennan, 1995, p. 59).

The TV networks closed each evening around 10.00 pm. At the El Rocco, this meant all the customers would leave so Arthur James was looking for ways to keep them around. At the suggestion of drummer Ralph Stock, the restaurant began hosting modern jazz performances and the El Rocco became a popular place to hear jazz in Sydney (Clare & Brennan, 1995, p. 60). The audience was a mix of professionals, musicians, academics and so-called beatniks (Clare & Brennan, 1995, p. 57). Trumpeter Colin Jones was among the regulars and recalled several others who frequented the club.

> We used to get all sorts of people in the Cross. It was very bohemian in those days. We even had Rosaleen Norton who was called the Witch of Kings Cross, Paul Rigby who was a cartoonist from Perth, and a sculptor there, who went to New York and became very successful, Clem Meadmore. It was a very cosmopolitan audience, a lot of young people, because we of course were young and our contemporaries would follow the music.

> (Jones, 2024)

Different jazz styles could be heard at the club because there were both old and young musicians performing and they had differing tastes (Clare & Brennan, 1995, p. 60). As the hard bop style led by Americans such as Art Blakey and the Jazz Messengers began to take hold in Australia, it found a home at El Rocco. The club also made room for improvisation, experimentation and modal jazz as the audiences were generally accepting of these explorations of modern jazz sounds. Many noted the coffee and food served was terrible quality and alcohol wasn't served at all. Consequently, it was the music alone which drew people in every evening (Clare & Brennan, 1995, p. 67).

Shortly after returning to Sydney in early 1960, Mike Nock had formed a quintet at El Rocco (El Rocco, 1960). The group, which could grow to a septet at times, included saxophonist Jimmie Sloggett, who remembered it well:

> We had trumpet and tenor as well as the rhythm section, Chris Karan. Bruce Edwards was the bass player for a while, and so was Bruce Cale. We were playing all kinds of stuff from the really great jazz quintets from around the world, depending on the records the guys had. I can't remember Mike playing any originals. Everyone wanted to only hear something that had been tried, tested, and proven, or recorded by somebody in the States and made a hit.
>
> (Sloggett, 2024)

The group played Sunday nights, and would then meet up again at 10.00 am Monday mornings to rehearse for the following Sunday. But after several months, the group broke up. As Sloggett recalled (Sloggett, 2024):

> Like all good things, they last for about three months and then it's all over. Because, in actual fact, Freddy Logan came along and pinched Mike Nock from his own band that us guys were in, and we were really saddened by that. But that was what happened those days. They formed The Three Out trio, and that was the end of our lovely three months with Mike Nock.
>
> (Sloggett, 2024)

3 Moving up: The Three Out

After seeing Mike Nock play at the El Rocco, Freddy Logan wanted to form a new trio with him. Then the question of who would play drums arose. Nock wanted Chris Karan to join them, but he was still under contract with the Rex Hotel, so was unavailable. Instead, English drummer Colin Bailey sat in and the trio rehearsed together until Karan was available.

Bailey had first visited Australia while on tour with pianist Winfred Atwell (Mckay, 2012). As previously mentioned, she had once been Mike Nock's favourite pianist (Clare & Brennan, 1995, p. 68). Bailey had joined Atwell's band in 1952 when he was eighteen and appeared on several of her recordings, though the band members were never credited. They toured Australia in 1955, 1956 and 1958. By which time Bailey had decided he wanted to play a different type of jazz and left Atwell's band (Mckay, 2012). In 1960, he was also a member of the Bryce Rohde Quartet, who would soon go on a tour performing jazz at Australian universities (Music Maker, 1960c). Consequently, it's unlikely Bailey would have been able to remain with The Three Out long. For Mike Nock, he wanted Chris Karan regardless:

> Colin Bailey was a great drummer. But I wanted to play with Chris. I was waiting for him. So, we started playing because Freddy saw something in me, and he saw a potential to have this group.
>
> (Nock, 2024)

The trio included Bailey only for a few weeks (Johnson, 1987, p. 148), before Chris Karan joined them by August 1960 (3-Out, 1961). They took the name The Three Out, possibly at the suggestion of Jazz Centre 44's Horst Liepolt, who was now in Sydney. El Rocco regular and trumpeter Colin Jones recalled:

> Horst Liepolt was always hovering about in the background. He had a lot to do with getting The Three Out started and encouraged them to get going. They were all keen, but they were all obviously doing other gigs elsewhere. Horst used to haunt the El Rocco, because they played down there quite regularly before they decided to formalise the formation and call it The Three Out, and I think he might have even come up with the name.
>
> (Jones, 2024)

Regardless of who came up with the name it would be remembered for decades to come.

The Three Out played modern jazz, with Nock's playing described by musician and writer Bruce Johnson as 'a type of jazz that took the music beyond its former limits' (Johnson, 1983a, p. 11). The trio proved popular within the Sydney jazz scene which quickly took notice and crowds filled the El Rocco to capacity (3-Out, 1961). Mike Nock later remembered some of their regulars:

> There was a woman called Babs who used to sort of moan and keen through the music, and there were these characters who'd get up in that tiny space and dance by themselves. Dancing by yourself was very unusual in those days. Something happened there. We'd be sweating heaps and there'd be all these people going apeshit over it. The club was like a church then. It was like a black gospel church. Everything was new. We felt like an élite.
>
> (Clare & Brennan, 1995, pp. 68–9)

Chris Karan recalled witnessing the excitement around the trio, as well as his own pleasure being part of it:

I think we made quite a bit of a sensation with the trio. There were people going crazy for the group and it was a terrific group to play in. Mike's music and the way he played was really quite rewarding for me because it got me going and put me on the right track for the way I should be playing. It was just so inspiring and rewarding, and I was really grateful for that.

(Karan, 2022a)

Nock's playing inspired many of the locals who would crowd the small club to listen to him. These included pianists like Dave Levy and Bobby Gebert, and bassist Rick Laird, who likened The Three Out to the Miles Davis Quintet's rhythm section of Red Garland, Paul Chambers and Philly Jo Jones (Meehan, 2010, p. 47).

Logan had his fans too. However, he stood out not just because of his skill but for the distinctive way he played. As noted earlier, Logan hadn't taken bass lessons until some five years after he'd started playing professionally in the Netherlands and Mike Nock said his unorthodox style was very unusual:

He played the bass like someone that couldn't play the bass, and I don't mean that in a negative way. It was like he was totally self-taught. He must have been, because he didn't play the bass like most bass players. I remember Freddy just kind of grabbing the bass in one hand. He was very rough and ready, but he had a great energy and he obviously had a lot of a musical ability and talent anyway.

(Nock, 2022)

Logan himself explained in 1958: 'The double bass is one of the most difficult instruments to play because of its size, and it scares taxi-drivers for the same reason, but I'm still glad I chose it' (Anon., 1958).

Among his fans, bassist Bruce Cale held Logan in high regard and considered him to be the best bassist of that period, even with his unorthodox style of playing. Cale explained (Cale, 2022):

> I used to be very intrigued with Freddy, as I started to study bass. He used the fingering that we used to refer to as the leg of mutton fingering. But he was such a good musician. When it came to his musicality, he would nail whatever he was playing. Also, the instrument he was playing was quite unusual. He had a five-string bass with a C string on the top, where he didn't go up the instrument, like any of the bassists of that era. Where they'd go into thumb position, he would just go over to his C string. And the instrument he had was horrible. He didn't have a cover for it, which meant the instrument was suffering from atmospheric problems. But that didn't seem to matter. I went along to El Rocco when they were playing there, and it was absolutely magical. And the beautiful thing with him was that he liked to get out of playing his gigs. So, he'd say, 'Come on, come and sit in, by all means.' And then he'd go with his whiskey bottle and have a few drinks. He was an unusual character, quite unusual for that era. I really looked up to him.
>
> (Cale, 2022)

Regardless of the way he held his bass, Logan was considered one of the best bassists in Australia at that point according to those who saw him as part of The Three Out and The Australian All-Stars. Both groups would soon be heard on forthcoming albums too. In December 1959, The Australian All-Stars had recorded their debut *Jazz for Beach-Niks* and it was released on 17 June 1960 to high praise. *Jazz Notes* wrote it was 'by far the best LP of modern jazz by a local group ever to be released here' (A.W.L., 1960). While *Music Maker* made the band their cover stars that month (The Australian Music Maker and Dance Band News, 1960) and reviewed the album favourably.

They highlighted Logan's 'graceful and velvety' bass which shone through extended solos on 'Strictly From Hunger' and 'Where and When' (Hart, 1960). Elsewhere, Logan's work on 'Strictly from Hunger' was given further praise, with *The Sun-Herald* writing, 'The laconic title doesn't do justice to the piece, an intriguing bass solo by Logan'. They concluded: 'This is an Australian jazz record you needn't be afraid to send overseas' and dubbed the All-Stars Australia's representatives of modern jazz (Downbeat, 1960c).

The album quickly became Australia's best-selling jazz record of the previous fourteen years, and was quickly followed by *Jazz for Beach-Niks Volume 2* in November 1960 (Downbeat, 1960b). *The Sun-Herald* noted the popularity of the Australian All-Stars first album and gave further praise to the second for aiding the development of an Australian sound (Downbeat, 1960b). Although musicians such as Don Burrows and Pat Caplice had released modern jazz albums by now, at the beginning of 1960 Australian modern jazz was still a rarity to find on record, as Jimmy Sloggett recalled:

> There was bugger all! We were thankful for the All-Stars, that they were even doing anything like they were, because there was not a lot happening in those days.

> (Sloggett, 2024)

Making *Move*

Since arriving in Australia in 1956, Freddy Logan had taken part in several jazz recordings for Columbia Records. The Music

Maker All Stars album was released by Columbia's sister label Parlophone, while his recordings with The Don Burrows Six, Ross Arno, The Australian All-Stars and The Loganberries had all been released by Columbia.

Nevertheless, even with his previous recording relationship with the label, it's an impressive feat that Logan, who acted as The Three Out's manager (Karan, 2022a), was able to secure a record deal for the trio within only a few months of them forming. This resulted in their debut album *Move*.

The Three Out entered Sydney's EMI recording studio on 28 September 1960 (Mitchell, 1988, p. 205) with plans for their album to be released by Columbia in mid-November (Lee Gordon, 1960a, p. 11). Session supervisor Eric Dunn had the trio play for two hours and recorded twenty-five songs before hearing any played back. Of those, Logan said they only liked five of the recordings and would need to come back to the studio to complete the album later (Music Maker, 1960d). They returned to the studio on 14 October (Mitchell, 1988, p. 205), recording a total of thirty different songs across the two sessions (Music Maker, 1960d). This pushed the expected release date to 'some time before Christmas' (Music Maker, 1960e). In the end, the album wouldn't be released until the following year.

Move features nine songs, of which three are originals. At the time, most Australian jazz performances were predominantly made up of American songs rather than originals. This carried over into those songs being recorded. The Three Out was no exception. The covering of American songs was done for two reasons: firstly, so local players could properly judge each other on how they played and interpreted popular jazz standards, and secondly, there was a belief that Australian composed jazz wasn't as good (Robson, 2021, p. 34). Of the jazz albums previously mentioned in this book by Pat Caplice, The Embers Quintet, The Music Maker All Stars and The Australian All-Stars, only The Music Maker All Stars contained a majority of Australian compositions. Three of the four songs were written by the musicians on that album. This balance of American and Australian compositions would change over the coming decades (Robson, 2021, p. 35) but in 1960 there were few new Australian jazz albums to choose from (Jones, 2024), and few Australian jazz musicians from this period made recordings compared to the abundance of recordings made and released by Americans (Page, 1997, p. 41). Outside of the lack of availability, jazz fans were also more likely to purchase an American jazz album than one by Australians. This was because Australian jazz was often considered too commercialised, designed to appeal to the widest market, compared to some of what came from America. It was only in jazz clubs like the El Rocco that there was an exception and where Australian jazz found a following (Page, 1997, p. 41).

In their live shows, The Three Out played a mixture of standards and originals, with Nock later recalling they played 'a lot of Horace Silver and Art Blakey' (Green, 1978). Neither Silver nor Blakey were represented on *Move*, but there were interpretations of other jazz greats.

Side-A of Move begins with 'Squeeze Me', originally performed by Duke Ellington as 'Subtle Slough'. It opens with Logan's bass soloing for the first ten seconds before Nock enters with Karan behind a moment later. The original had been written by Ellington in 1941 and recorded by Miles Davis in 1956 as 'Just Squeeze Me' (SecondHandSongs, 2025c). Most of these renditions differ from The Three Out's by having a trumpet or vocals. Because of this, The Three Out's version sounds more stripped back than previous recordings and is also performed at a faster pace. This recording was made at the trio's September session, and was the second take (Music Maker, 1960d).

'If I Were a Bell' had become a jazz standard thanks to its inclusion on Miles Davis's 1958 album *Relaxin' with the Miles Davis Quintet*. It was originally written for the 1950 musical *Guys and Dolls* by composer Frank Loesser. The Three Out performed their version much faster than Davis. While Davis's version runs eight minutes, The Three Out's is less than five.

'Primitive', a Logan original, is another from the September sessions (Music Maker, 1960d). It opens with just bass and drums before Nock's piano joins in. The song is initially fairly repetitive, with Logan playing the same rhythm for almost two minutes before Nock's piano lowers in volume to allow a bass solo. Then the piano becomes louder for a moment to reassert itself before pulling back as Karan performs his own drum solo, with Logan and Nock gently repeating their rhythms in the back. After repeating the opening section together, the band fade out completely. The song is notable for being in a 5/4 time signature. Something Nock said was considered a big deal at the time:

> I'd never played in anything except 4/4, maybe 3/4, my entire life. So, I remember I had to play counting all the time with one finger on one hand … it was quite challenging, but hey, you jumped in and you did it anyway.
>
> (Presley, 2016)

'Way Back' is the only song credited to the entire trio. Recorded at the second session in October, it is slower paced than the album's early tracks and features another extended solo from Logan. But it's the piano that is the real focus of 'Way Back'. It opens with a piano solo and is notable as the first time Mike Nock's own composition was heard on record.

'Move' ends Side-A of the album, and is another song recorded previously by Miles Davis. Written by Denzil Best, it appeared on Davis's *Birth of the Cool*, and is fast and short, with both Davis's and The Three Out's renditions running just over two minutes in length. They differ thanks to the lack of a horn section in The Three Out but otherwise both versions follow the same beats, down to Karan's percussion mimicking Max Roach's original. 'Move' was first released by Davis in 1949 but its inclusion on *Birth of the Cool* album in 1957, close to a decade later, meant it was still fresh in the ears of modern jazz fans. Notably, Davis's recording of 'Move' had been cited by Logan in 1951 as an example of how modern jazz has continued to evolve (Loggen, 1951). Its inclusion on *Move* suggests it clearly remained a favourite for him almost ten years later. But while Davis's 'Move' ends suddenly and without warning, The Three Out extend their outro to wrap it up neatly as Side-A of their album ends.

Side-B begins with 'Softly as in a Morning Sunrise', originally written for the 1928 opera *The New Moon*. Pianist Vince Guaraldi had released his take in 1958, as had John Coltrane and Sonny Clark, Sonny Rollins and Paul Chambers (SecondHandSongs, 2025b), while Oscar Peterson included it in his live shows (3-Out, 1961). Peterson had toured Australia earlier in 1960 and The Three Out had seen him play at The Embers in Melbourne, sitting front row each night (Karan, 2022b). In his liner notes to *Move*, Australian All-Stars pianist Terry Wilkinson cited the tour as influencing The Three Out's rendition of 'Softly as in a Morning Sunrise' (3-Out, 1961) and Nock had been upfront that he played in a Peterson-like style at this time (Meehan, 2010, p. 48). When the trio saw Peterson in Melbourne, Chris Karan was also very impressed with his drummer Ed Thigpen. He recalled:

> I loved the way he played, and when I heard him I thought, 'God! That's how you should sound in a trio of that idiom'. Ed was perfect, and he was a big influence on my playing. We kept in touch for many years, and when we went back to the Rocco he came in to hear the trio and really enjoyed it.
>
> (Karan, 2022b)

'Little Niles', written by pianist Randy Weston, was first recorded in 1956 for Weston's album *With These Hands* … released that year. Then he recorded it again in 1958 for an album of the same name released in 1959. The Three Out's version is perhaps closest to the original, though Nock has added his own interpretation. The trio perform it faster than the original as has become clear is their style. Randy Weston later told Nock he was 'knocked out' by the song's inclusion on *Move* (Presley, 2016).

'Freshwater', another Logan original, was also recorded in 1960 by Logan's other group The Australian All-Stars for their album *Jazz For Beach-Niks Volume 2*. Although it's clearly the same song, the All-Stars version seems overcrowded in comparison as the five musicians crowd the mix. In comparison, The Three Out version is much more restrained and allows each member of the trio to solo and give impact to the piece which is primarily a back and forth between Logan and Nock. The title came from Freshwater Beach in Sydney (Logan, 1965). It is located north of Manly in a suburb that was known as Harbord at the time but was renamed Freshwater in 2008 (Morcombe, 2021). When asked his thoughts on the All-Stars' version, Mike Nock admitted in 2024 he hadn't been aware of it until told: 'I haven't heard that one. That's how ignorant, or self-obsessed,

I am. I try not to be' (Nock, 2024). Logan later revived the song in 1965 when he performed it with his Afro-Cuban Orchestra (Logan, 1965).

'Autumn in New York' is the final song on the album. It was written by Vernon Duke in 1934 and became a jazz standard, subsequently performed and recorded by Charlie Parker, Oscar Peterson, Billie Holiday and Sonny Stitt (SecondHandSongs, 2025a). Logan had also recorded the song previously with Tommy Whittle in 1956. In The Three Out's version, the song starts out much slower than the rest of the album's pace. Although it picks up, it never takes off at the speed that much of Side-A displayed, allowing Nock to show off a more restrained side. Then, just as you expect things to pick up, the trio pull back and Logan's bass takes over as Nock plays softly to the point he almost completely disappears behind his bandmates, before coming back to the foreground as they end the album together. The final note heard is from Nock's piano, sustained a moment by itself before cutting out and *Move* ends.

While recording the album, The Three Out continued to play the El Rocco until concert promoter Lee Gordon convinced the group to leave and start playing at his nearby strip club The Primitif on Bayswater Road (Lee Gordon, 1960a, p. 11). It was this move that almost had their debut album named *Jazz at the Primitif*, according to a note on the master tapes (National Film and Sound Archive of Australia, 1960). Clearly a fan of the trio, Gordon then invited The Three Out to be part of a national jazz tour he was planning. On the same night Gordon heard them Australian singer Diana Trask also invited the trio to join her next US tour (Lee Gordon, 1960a, p. 11). Trask had previously sung with the Australian All-Stars at the Sky Lounge (Downbeat, 1960d). Freddy Logan had backed her when she supported Frank Sinatra on his 1959 Australian tour (Hart, 1959).

After that, Trask had left Australia and begun building a career in the United States. At the end of July 1961, she returned for a short tour (Feldman, 1961) and must have found time to see The Three Out. Unfortunately for Trask, the trio elected to stay in Australia for the time being. However, this meant they'd be available for Lee Gordon's tour instead.

The First Australian International Jazz Festival

Lee Gordon had arrived in Australia from the United States in 1953 and began a series of tours featuring American artists that he called The Big Show (Apter & Hill, 2025). Early visitors included Ella Fitzgerald, Nat 'King Cole and Bill Hailey. Australian artists occasionally supported the Americans (Apter, 2025, pp. 202–4). However, this wasn't common until Johnny O'Keefe appeared on a tour with Little Richard in 1957. Following the success of O'Keefe's appearance Gordon began to include more Australian acts alongside Americans and he helped launch the careers of people such as O'Keefe and Diana Trask (Apter & Hill, 2025). The success of O'Keefe also shifted Gordon's focus during the 1950s towards rock and in particular shows that were marketed towards teenagers (Apter, 2025, p. 86). This would change in 1960 when Gordon decided to put on what he called 'the biggest jazz show ever put together anywhere in the world' (Heffernan, 2003, p. 366).

The First Australian International Jazz Festival ran from 26 to 29 October 1960 with concerts in Adelaide, Brisbane, Melbourne and Sydney (Lee Gordon, 1960a). A group named 'Australian Jazz All Stars' were originally advertised as appearing at the festival (Lee Gordon, 1960b), before The Three Out replaced them on the bill two weeks later (Lee Gordon, 1960c). This perhaps suggests that Logan's other group The Australian All-Stars were originally intended to appear. Alongside The Three Out, the international artists on the tour were musicians Dizzy Gillespie, Coleman Hawkins, Jonah Jones Quartet and the Teddy Wilson Trio, with singers Al Hibbler, Gene McDaniels, Dakota Staton and Sarah Vaughan. Australian's The Bryce Rohde Quartet were also on the bill (Lee Gordon, 1960a). The festival ran for four days, with the artists split up into two groups and performing in different cities simultaneously. The Three Out appeared on the same bill as Staton, McDaniels, Hawkins and the Teddy Wilson Trio. Their leg of the tour began in Adelaide, then travelled to Melbourne, Brisbane and Sydney (De Looper, 2024).

The Sydney Sunday Telegraph were fans of The Three Out and wrote of their Sydney set that 'the group contributed a lot more and a lot better jazz than some of the American artists. It's members are not cool, cerebral, and way-out, they're hard-hitting, hot and swinging' (NZ Listener, 1962). Their tour partners also praised The Three Out, with Teddy Wilson calling them 'one of the best jazz trios I've heard', while Dakota Staton said of Freddy Logan, 'Logan is exceptional. I would like to see him come to America where there is great demand for players of his calibre.' Both quotes were later used to promote The Three Out on tour (Civic Theatre, 1961).

Alongside their own set, The Three Out also played together as Gene McDaniels's band and sat in with other international guests as needed. Logan and Karan supported Dakota Staton and the Coleman Hawkins Quartet (Various, 1960), while Karan also sat in with Teddy Wilson after his drummer had to go back to the United States (Karan, 2022a). Karan recalled:

> It was nice being with Coleman Hawkins. He didn't say a lot,
> but he played a lot. It was really nice of Lee Gordon to put

this on because it was the very first international one that had happened in Australia. It's just a shame it wasn't filmed. That would have been terrific.

(Karan, 2022a)

Likewise, Nock was blown away that they were able to play with musicians of such international recognition in Australia. He commented:

> It was quite incredible actually. The little Three Out trio on the stage with people like Dizzy Gillespie and Coleman Hawkins. And we toured everywhere in the country to huge numbers of people. It was bizarre. And that's why people remember The Three Out, I'm sure. That plus the little record that sold a few copies. It made me feel a certain way about myself, I guess. In a very positive way. It gave me confidence. And I felt that even when I was in the States, that I was as good as anybody. It doesn't mean to say I think I played as well as anybody, I'm not saying that! But I felt the equal of everybody.

(Nock, 2024)

Recordings of the festival were made for later broadcast on ABC radio, with twelve thirty-minute episodes broadcast in 1961. The first included a set by The Three Out (The Australian Women's Weekly, 1961). Unfortunately, these are no longer held by the ABC Archives (Archives, 2022). Other recordings are scarce, with a short silent video of the Sydney show held by the National Film and Sound Archive (Isackson, 1960) and an audio recording of some Adelaide shows held by The Australian Jazz Museum (Australian Jazz Museum, n.d.). The latter can also be found on YouTube (Music for Your Ears, 2023).

On the recordings from Adelaide, The Three Out open with a cover of Miles Davis's 'Milestones' and later perform 'Birks'

Works' by Dizzy Gillespie. The rest of their set was made up of songs they'd recorded for *Move*, mostly from the album's B-side: 'Softly as in a Morning Sunrise', 'Little Niles', 'Freshwater' and 'Move' (Various, 1960).

Peter Cawthorne, who promoted and produced jazz concerts in Adelaide, hosted these shows. He told the audience ahead of their performance that he had heard a preview of The Three Out album. He described it as 'the best Australian jazz disc I've heard' and said it would be released later that year. He then voiced his disappointment at the small crowd in attendance, telling those who did turn up: 'I think personally this is one of the most fantastic shows value wise, artist wise, that we have had the opportunity of seeing anywhere' (Various, 1960). Similar views were shared by those who attended the shows in Melbourne and Sydney.

In Melbourne, Myke Dyer wrote for *Jazz Notes* that there was low attendance there also, 'but those who turned up were very enthusiastic about the great jazz sounds'. He felt The Three Out's performance proved great Australian jazz was being played and that the festival did a good job of promoting the presentation of 'good jazz' to an increasingly interested audience (Dyer, 1960). Members of the Canberra Jazz Club reviewed the Sydney shows and found The Three Out 'a really good modern jazz group who play their music precisely but with a fresh, brilliant rhythm'. Bruce Lansley compared the experience between attending the jazz shows and a rock and roll show and wrote the difference was 'staggering': 'No bad traffic jams extending to King's Cross, no milling teenagers overflowing onto the roadway, and not all seats filled for the show itself' (Ford et al., 1960). To the surprise of many of the attendees, the Sydney show began one hour early so several people missed the opening acts, which included The Three Out. John Ford did see them and wrote:

> [The Three Out are] certainly out, but nonetheless controlled, expressive and jazz. These three complement to the end, and are naturals. The most striking feature of all, is Karan's anticipation, and his background rhythm counterpoint to the solo bits, vocal and instrumental.
>
> (Ford et al., 1960)

Though it was mostly seen as a success by those who attended (Ford et al., 1960), the festival as a whole was unsuccessful, with only small crowds turning out in each city. Those who did come could be restless, with Dizzy Gillespie heckled in Adelaide (Various, 1960) and Sydney (Lawson & Somerville, 1960). To the press, Lee Gordon insisted the tour had been a success and would return in 1961 as a week-long Sydney Jazz Festival. Sarah Vaughan was said to have already signed on to return (Lawson & Somerville, 1960). However, behind the scenes things weren't going so well.

At the end of 1960, Lee Gordon had made a £200,000 loss thanks to the jazz festival (Heffernan, 2003, p. 368). In an attempt to make some money back, Gordon sent Sarah Vaughan and Dizzy Gillespie to New Zealand (Heffernan, 2003, p. 367) for what was billed as New Zealand's First Annual International Festival of Jazz 1960 (National Library Wellington, 1960). In Australia, Gordon booked several of the artists for his Pigalle Theatre Restaurant (Lee Gordon, 1960d) including The Three Out and Gene McDaniels (Lawson & Somerville, 1960). The Three Out and McDaniels also appeared on *Some Jazz in Australia*, a TV special additionally featuring Teddy Wilson, Dakota Staton, Barbara Virgil and the Bryce Rohde Quartet. It aired in February 1961 (The Sydney Morning Herald, 1961), reminding people of the Annual Australian International Jazz Festival which was never repeated.

Before the festival, The Three Out had left the El Rocco and moved to The Primitif, but Mike Nock wasn't happy because the audience gave all their attention to the strip shows rather than the band. 'I'm used to having people listen to me. I want people to listen, otherwise why do it? I don't get it', he said (Nock, 2024). Before the year ended, The Three Out moved venues again, this time to The Hungry I, run by Lee Sharon, who had previously managed The Primitif until she broke off her engagement with Lee Gordon and started her own restaurant (The Bulletin, 1961). Opening in December 1960, The Three Out and Abe Jenson Trio were the house bands.

Owner Ian Kennedy later recounted the opening night. This had been set to feature singer Gene McDaniels (Kennedy & Courtenay, 1995, pp. 119–24). There were 1,000 people lining up to get into the 250-capacity restaurant. Then the head chef walked out for a packet of cigarettes and never returned:

> By 8 p.m., I was in a state of panic. The place was packed to the rafters: people were banging on the tables demanding food. Downstairs, I had two kitchen hands who probably couldn't boil water. Fortunately, the music was good and the mood of the crowd held and they drank enough grog to temporarily forget that they were hungry.

After requisitioning a chef from his other restaurant, the Café Inferno, Kennedy was met by Detective Sergeant O'Leary from Darlinghurst police station, a member of the Drug Squad. O'Leary asked whether Gene McDaniels was scheduled to play that evening. He then revealed he had just put McDaniels back onto a plane for the United States: 'Sorry son, we caught him with some of that marijuana in his possession and the commissioner thought, rather than make, like a fuss, him being a Yank an' all, we'd just quietly put him on a plane back to America.' The night was saved when singer Nancy Wilson arrived hoping to see Gene McDaniels.

After Kennedy explained what had happened, she offered to sing instead. In Kennedy's words:

> Nancy Wilson sat under a spotlight and the crowd hushed as the Three Out Trio fingered the opening bars to 'Bye, Bye, Blackbird' and then the crowd simply went berserk, Nancy sang her heart out without a break for nearly two hours and the Hungry I Jazz Club was not only saved but became famous overnight.
>
> (Kennedy & Courtenay, 1995, pp. 119–24)

However, The Three Out didn't last at the Hungry I. According to Lee Sharon, it was because they wanted to play modern jazz:

> The Three Out are out. I told them that people couldn't dance to their music. They said they played real jazz you know, far out. Fine, I said, I like that stuff, too, but do me a favor and go play it someplace else. The customers have to dance, don't they?
>
> (The Bulletin, 1961)

By February, the trio had moved back to the El Rocco (Lawson & Somerville, 1961a), where they played Tuesday to Friday from 9.00 pm. Saturday featured the Warren Leroy Trio. The Bob Gillette [*sic*] Quartet played Sunday and the club closed Monday (Music Maker, 1960f). Gillett's group had initially featured guitarist Lennie Hutchinson, bassist Rick Laird, drummer Tony Hopkins and Gillett on saxophone. But when Hopkins left, he was replaced by Chris Karan, and then Mike Nock joined too (Lawson, 1961). This meant that at the start of

1961 each of The Three Out now had a regular gig on Sundays with Logan at the Sky Lounge.

There were seemingly more chances than ever to see The Three Out perform in Sydney and it wasn' much longer until their debut album *Move* would finally be released too. Before then, The Three Out had made another recording in 1960 with singer Bruce Gillespie, though they were left uncredited.

Gillespie was originally from India and had arrived in Australia in 1956 when he was fourteen years old. He appeared on TV programmes *Bandstand* and *Six O'Clock Rock*, and made a name for himself around Sydney clubs where he sang in a style reminiscent of Nat 'King' Cole (Teenager's Weekly, 1960). He recorded his debut single 'Velvet Waters' in Sydney with a band made up of The Three Out along with guitarist Peter Beasley, vibraphonist Abe Jensen, and additional vocals by The Delltones (Gillespie, 2025). 'Velvet Waters' was released by HMV and entered the charts on 27 August 1960. It spent fourteen weeks there before dropping out in December. It reached a peak of #29 in the national Kent Report, #27 in Brisbane, #16 in Sydney, and #7 in Hobart. In Sydney it was the 98th highest selling song of 1960 (Ryan, 2024). Gillespie released two more singles recorded with Bruce Clarke, though neither charted. These were his final recordings and Gillespie retired from music in 1978 (Nuttall, 2025). The 'Velvet Waters' session was mostly forgotten, and when asked, neither Mike Nock nor Chris Karan had any recollection of it at all (Nock & Karan, 2025). However, Bruce Gillespie is certain it was them on his session (Gillespie, 2025). For The Three Out, they could be forgiven for forgetting it had occurred because, as this chapter has made clear, a lot had happened for the trio in 1960. However, they would only get busier in the new year.

4   Moving out: The impact of *Move*

After a long wait for jazz fans around Australia, *Move* was released on vinyl in stereo and mono in March 1961 (De Looper, 2025a, p. 75). The cover photograph was taken by the Australian sculptor Clement Meadmore, who had been a regular at the El Rocco. He was also responsible for the album design featuring a stark black-and-white photo of the trio performing in shadows against orange text: 'The Three Out', with the album title in lowercase (3-Out, 1961). Nock referred to the look of the cover as 'jazz noir' and suggested this was a major reason for *Move*'s appeal (Presley, 2016).

In their review, *The Sun-Herald* highlighted 'Freshwater' and spoke highly of Logan in general, writing: 'Logan, as a bassist, is the best we have heard here. He has worked tirelessly for modern jazz both on the stand and off it, in the organising of groups, dates, and support for his music.' Elsewhere they praised Nock's piano playing as being 'virile and commanding' but noted he sometimes would 'lapse into the Oscar Peterson style of playing' (Downbeat, 1961a). This is something Nock likely would have taken as a compliment, as he later described his work with The Three Out as him patterning himself after Bobby Timmons and Oscar Peterson (Green, 1978).

Overseas, Ron Tudor, Australian correspondent for American magazine *Cashbox*, wrote about *Move* soon after its release, 'Albums of this nature can do a lot for Australian jazz overseas and this record should easily find an overseas market'

(Tudor, 1961). However, although copies would eventually find their way overseas thanks to collectors, The Three Out never released an album outside of Australia and in 1961 seemed content touring Australia during gaps in their residency at El Rocco. Still, *Move* sold over 3,000 copies (Sharpe, 2008, p. 145) and both the mono and stereo pressings were repressed by Columbia as part of their Encore Series (3-Out, n.d.). Later, Nock revealed it was his most successful recording for 'many, many years' (Presley, 2016). Nevertheless, while *Move* had many fans, Nock wasn't one of them:

> The thing is, I could hardly play the piano, to be really honest. I mean, I had spirit and energy and all that, but I was really, really, really rough. However, having said that, the first record was the one that was by far more successful. It really ignited some kind of interest in people, and I'm not sure why. I really had no technique whatsoever and I'm just doing the best I can. But it seems some resonated with that.
>
> (Nock, 2022)

Pianist Ted Nettelbeck had been a fan of Nock's since they first met in 1959 and bought *Move* as soon as it came out. He said:

> I remember 'Little Niles', I learnt that tune from the album actually, and I thought Mike was a great piano player. If he thought he was rough at that time, goodness knows what he thought of me, because he was a much better player than anyone of us really.
>
> (Nettelbeck, 2022)

In the album liner notes, Terry Wilkinson praised Karan and Nock as two names that 'stand out above the rest', who had 'risen from obscurity to the top of the ladder' thanks to their devotion to music. He then singled out Logan's impact on

Australian jazz, writing: 'Due to an aptitude for promotion he has done more good for the advancement and recognition of modern jazz than anybody in Australia' (3-Out, 1961). The Three Out would often be cited over the coming decades as an important part of Australian jazz history (Jackson, 1979), and it was *Move* which secured their legacy. Jazz musician and journalist Dick Hughes later championed *Move* as 'one of the greatest jazz recordings ever made in Australia' (Hughes, 1980). As did journalist Eric Myers, who similarly described it as `one of the classic albums in Australian jazz history' recorded by `the top jazz group in the country' The Three Out (Myers, 1981).

Move wasn't the first album of Australian modern jazz. That honour was given to vibraphonist Pat Caplice with his album *Caprice: Adventures in Sound with Pat Caplice*, considered the first jazz album by an Australian group on the then-new 12" format (The Sydney Morning Herald, 1958). Caplice's album was in the 'cool jazz' style (Downbeat, 1958) and overseas it was likened to a 'cocktail lounge jazz group which occasionally echoes the sound of the Modern Jazz Quartet' (Morgan, 1959). The Embers Quintet and Australian All-Stars had followed with their respective albums in 1960, as had The Bryce Rohde Quartet, who recorded and released their debut album relatively quickly compared to The Three Out. While The Three Out finished recording in October 1960 (Mitchell, 1988, p. 205) and released *Move* in March 1961 (De Looper, 2025a, p. 75), The Bryce Rohde Quartet recorded their album in August 1960 (Mitchell, 1988, p. 183) and released it in October that same year (De Looper, 2014, p. 21).

Pianist Bryce Rohde had found success during the 1950s in the United States with his group The Australian Jazz Quartet/Quintet, but they had broken up after returning to Australia. Rohde then formed The Bryce Rohde Quartet with bassist

Ed Gaston, guitarist George Golla and drummer Colin Bailey (Bisset, 1987, pp. 103–4, 144). They had performed at El Rocco the same time as The Mike Nock Quintet in early 1960 (El Rocco, 1960) and Bailey had been an original member of The Three Out, as discussed earlier (Nock, 2022), so there would be some crossover between the two groups and their followings. The Bryce Rohde Quartet had also joined Lee Gordon's jazz festival in October 1960, accompanying Company A, where they supported Americans such as Dizzy Gillespie, while The Three Out were on Company B (De Looper, 2024, p. 27).

During the festival The Bryce Rohde Quartet had released their debut album *In Concert* (Various, 1960). The album was seen as a departure from Rohde's work with The Australian Jazz Quintet (Downbeat, 1960e). One review wrote *In Concert* was 'Interesting without being scary' (Baker, 1960a). While Rohde described the group's style as 'not far out' with a commercial appeal that would interest the average person (Baker, 1960b).

It's impossible to say whether *In Concert* was more commercially successful than *Move* as no sales data from their two record labels appears to have been published. Likewise, the Australian music charts at the time were based on songs being played on the radio. The national ARIA chart began in the late 1980s and included jazz albums as well as other genre specific charts (O'Regan & Byron, 2024, pp. 149, 150). However, in the 1960s the charts tended to focus on pop music and songs by The Three Out and The Bryce Rohde Quartet didn't appear in them (Ryan, 2024).

While they may not have been taking the charts by storm, even before *Move* was released The Three Out had built a reputation outside of Sydney. During their appearance at Lee Gordon's jazz festival in Adelaide, host Peter Cawthorne introduced The Three Out as 'three Sydney boys well known to many of us'. He added they were the only Australian jazz group, to his knowledge, playing jazz full-time in Australia, while other local artists were putting in the effort but for little financial return (Various, 1960).

Although there were other Australian jazz trios at the time, The Three Out were the only modern jazz trio to record an album. What set them further apart from the other Australia jazz being recorded was their instrumentation. The Pat Caplice Quartet, who recorded 1958's *Caprice* album, featured vibraphone, bass, flute and guitar. The Embers Quintet featured bass, drums, alto and tenor saxophone, piano and vocals. The Australian All-Stars's debut album featured clarinet, flute, baritone and tenor saxophone, bass, drums and piano, while The Bryce Rohde Quartet featured piano, bass, guitar and drums.

In comparison, The Three Out featured piano, bass and drums, with no reed or wind instruments. This simplified sound allowed Nock's piano in particular to stand out. Compare the trio's recording of 'Freshwater' on *Move* with the version on The Australian All-Stars's album *Jazz for Beach-Niks Volume 2*. The latter is led by saxophone and flute with the piano and bass very much in the background. In contrast, The Three Out's version puts all of the focus on Nock's piano and Logan's bass, turning it into one of the album's highlights (Downbeat, 1961a).

When The Three Out performed live, they didn't stray from their trio format. While some groups might let others sit in with them, this wasn't something The Three Out allowed. Mike Nock recalled:

> I don't remember that happening with The Three Out, and I'd
> be surprised, as our gigs were pretty intense and you'd have
> to be pretty brave to get up and play with us.

(Nock, 2024)

Back in December 1960, the trio had performed on *Six O'Clock Rock* (The Age, 1960), and returned to TV on 5 March 1961 with an appearance on *Revue 61* (The Sun-Herald, 1961) before they commenced a short interstate tour (Lawson & Somerville, 1961b). Beginning with two shows at University of NSW on 3 March (Lawson & Somerville, 1961b), the trio then went down to Melbourne as part of the Coca Cola HiFi Club Jazz Concert on 10 March at Sidney Myer Music Bowl (Lee, 1961). The Three Out were flown from Sydney especially for this event by Coca Cola and performed 'Tune Up', 'Moanin', 'This Here', 'Night in Tunisia, and 'Blues by Five', with several encores extending their set out further (Lee, 1961). They remained in Melbourne for additional shows at the Basin Street Jazz Centre which were said to be less inhibited. Their performance of 'The Hucklebuck' was described as 'amazingly fresh, due mainly to lively bass soloing and close ensemble leads with some sensitive off-beat cymbal work'. Other songs included 'Anthropology', 'How High The Moon', 'No Greater Love' and 'Little Niles', with the latter considered the most moving part of their set due to its haunting chorus and unusual intervals (Rawlins, 1961).

Next, they performed in Canberra on 13 March, billed as 'The Revolutionary 3-out Trio' (The Canberra Jazz Club, 1961), then returned to *Six O'Clock Rock* on 18 March as the featured jazz group (Lawson & Somerville, 1961b). They were on the programme again on 1 April billed as Freddy Logan and The Three Out Trio (The Toowoomba Chronicle, 1961). April saw the trio briefly back at the El Rocco (Music Maker, 1961) until they left Australia for a short tour of New Zealand organized by Ray Bolwell (Langlands, 2022). Arriving on 17 April 1961 (The Press, 1961), the trio were accompanied by the Australian singer Paula Langlands, who was dating and went on to marry Bolwell (Langlands, 2022). She recalled the tour well:

> It was only [two shows], with a recording session for New Zealand's equivalent of our ABC, which was somewhat of a disaster. The studio was not weather proof and the settings set for the trio in the morning were a mess in the afternoon after lunch. By the time the balance was reset there was only time to record two songs. We were all good friends, and I had worked with Freddy and Chris independently on other gigs in Sydney. Freddy was a first call bassist in Sydney at that time, quite liked generally, but perhaps a little quiet. Terri King said she was in love with him and I must confess to a bit of a crush too.
>
> (Langlands, 2022)

The tour opened in Wellington the night the trio arrived and then went to Christchurch two days later to perform at The Civic Centre (The Press, 1961). In their review of The Three Out's performance in Christchurch, *Press* wrote it was an enjoyable show, with well-chosen material, including 'Little Niles' and Miles Davis's 'Flamenco Sketches':

> Nock had many inspired moments and managed to create some memorable and inspired music; Freddy Logan filled his role as harmonic pacemaker with aplomb, and Chris Karan roamed freely and fully over his drum kit but kept up a tight, driving rhythm that helped to knit the group together.
>
> (D.W.R., 1961)

A third show in Auckland had been scheduled to end the tour, but was cancelled only two days before, due to a double booking being made at the venue. Instead, Nock spent time jamming with local musicians Kim Paterson (Meehan, 2010, p. 50), Bill Brown and Mike Williams, much to their delight (Warren, 1961).

While Paula Langlands recalled only two songs being recorded for radio during this tour, *New Zealand Listener* later reported the trio had recorded six programmes for the New Zealand Broadcasting Service (NZ Listener, 1962). These were aired in March 1962 across the country, with *New Zealand Listener* writing, 'Each programme is balanced musically and is sure to appeal to more than the ardent jazz follower … Australian vocalist Paula Langlands joins the group for the occasional number' (NZ Listener, 1962). No recordings appear to have survived.

At the time there was talk in the media of The Three Out touring the United States (The Press, 1961), and Mike Nock was certainly still looking for his ticket there. Earlier, he had made a recording of four songs during a radio session with Chris Karan and bassist Rick Laird and sent them to the American music magazine *Down Beat* (not to be confused with *The Sun-Herald*'s music column Downbeat) as entry to their annual scholarship programme (Fisher & Somerville, 1961a).

While awaiting news of the scholarship, The Three Out returned to the studio and recorded their second album *Sittin' In* on 2, 3 and 10 May 1961. It featured guests Errol Buddle, Don Burrows, Ron Falson and Colin Jones sitting in with the trio on the album's B-side (Mitchell, 1988, p. 205). Before they entered the studio, saxophonist Graham Lyall was said to be possibly taking part in the sessions (Lawson & Somerville, 1961c). However, he ultimately didn't appear on the album.

Of those who did appear, Don Burrows and Ron Falson had previously recorded with Freddy Logan on the two Australian All-Stars albums. Burrows had the most recording experience of anyone in the sessions. He'd left school at fifteen to play clarinet in Sydney's nightclubs and made his first recording the next year in 1944. These were with George Trevare's Jazz

Group in the swing style (Shand, 2020). Then in 1956 Burrows released *Music for Moderns*, the first record under his own name (Discogs, 2025c). A prolific multi-instrumentalist, Don Burrows released his final album in 2015. He died in 2020 (Shand, 2020).

Born in Clovelly, New South Wales, Ron Falson had begun playing trumpet at the age of fourteen and went on to study the instrument at the Sydney Conservatorium (Heathcote, 2008). During the 1940s and 1950s, he was playing at several clubs around Sydney (Myers, n.d.). With the advent of television in Australia in 1956 his group, the Ron Falson Quintet, appeared regularly on people's screens (Heathcote, 2008). When Lee Gordon began bringing American artists to Australia, Falson was regularly part of the pit band and often took his camera with him to document the shows. His interest in photography extended to creating artwork for some of his bandmates, including Don Burrows and Graeme Bell (Myers, n.d.) and also the two albums from The Australian All-Stars, of which he was a member. He died in 2008 (Heathcote, 2008).

Errol Buddle was born in Adelaide and, after performing in dance bands across Australia, relocated to Canada in 1952 where he later reconnected with two Adelaide friends and musicians, drummer Jack Brokensha and pianist Bryce Rohde. Together with American bassist Dick Healey they formed the Australian Jazz Quartet. This became the Australian Jazz Quintet after Healey moved to flute and Australian Jack Lander filled his role on bass. They toured across the United States until returning to Australia in 1958 (Myers, 2018), where they broke up (Dean et al., 2025). For the recording of *Sittin' In* in 1961, Buddle contributed tenor sax. While this was said to be his primary instrument (Shand, 2018) he performed with fourteen different reed instruments across his career (McBeath, 2015) from bassoons to clarinets (Shand, 2018). He died in 2018 (Myers, 2018).

Colin Jones was born in Byron Bay, where he first played with a local brass band. He studied trumpet at the Sydney Conservatorium (Mr Kokomo, n.d.) and met Freddy Logan at Jazz Club 11, where they both performed. Jones had his first professional gigs touring Australia with English rock and roll star Tommy Steele, alongside several of the Jazz Club 11 regulars, including Logan. Following the tour, Jones began spending time in Sydney's jazz clubs where he met Mike Nock and they performed together at El Rocco until Jones took a job at another club, Chequers. Although he performed regularly, *Sittin' In* is one of Colin Jones's few recording sessions (Jones, 2024). He explained:

> That's the only session I got to play with the big guys. They were just going to do it with Falson on trumpet but then Mike talked them into putting me in on it. I would have been 26 when I recorded with them. When we were in the studio, we hadn't seen any of the songs. Well, I hadn't. So, we ran them through before we recorded them, and all of them were one-takes apart from 'Loganberries' which had a second take. But all the other takes were what came out on the LP.
>
> (Jones, 2024)

While he hadn't been a fan of their debut, Mike Nock felt his playing on *Sittin' In* had improved as his style matured:

> A few years ago, I heard what I wasn't hearing. There's no question to me that my actual piano playing was much better on that, and it's still a long way from where I'd like it to be, but it was a lot better than it was on the first record.
>
> (Nock, 2024)

Sittin' In is notable for being the first album to feature a song composed entirely by Nock (Robson, 2021, p. 34). In fact, there are two Nock originals, 'New Jade' and 'Dizzy Pipe'. Logan also contributed an original 'Nock Out', as did Burrows and Falson, with the B-side containing all originals and the A-side three standards alongside Nock's 'New Jade'.

With the album recorded and awaiting release, The Three Out were continuing to play at El Rocco (Lawson & Somerville, 1961c) when *Down Beat* announced Mike Nock would receive their Hall of Fame Scholarship, including $200 and study at the Berklee School of Music in Boston (Down Beat, 1961). With the news of Nock's scholarship confirmed, The Three Out left Australia on a three-month European tour and Logan organized for the band to perform on the RHMS *Patris* in exchange for their tickets (Nock, 2024). The boat was capable of carrying over 1,000 passengers (McFadzean & Churchward, 2009) and The Three Out were free to play their own music for their audience (Meyer, 2024). Departing Sydney on May 16 for Athens (RHMS Patris, 1961b), they would have spent close to a month at sea after which passengers could take a train onwards to England (RHMS Patris, 1961a). This was all thanks to Freddy Logan. Mike Nock explained:

> Freddy was very good at organising and he would have organised the free passage to England. They had a Greek band, and then they had us to play at the parties outside. We didn't play in the main dining room, but it was a free passage, are you kidding me! It was a fantastic experience.
>
> (Nock, 2024)

Before leaving, Nock joined The Australian All-Stars briefly while Terry Wilkinson took a holiday in Queensland (Lawson & Somerville, 1961d). After Freddy Logan left, The Australian All-Stars continued to play together each Sunday with Logan initially replaced by Rick Laird and then John Allen (Fisher &

Somerville, 1961b). The original lineup appeared together on the cover of *Music Maker*'s July 1961 issue, by which time Logan was no longer in the country.

With The Three Out gone, others stepped in to replace them (Lawson & Somerville, 1961d) and pianist Dick Hughes later wrote that the local Sydney jazz scene in 1961 was the healthiest it had been since the late 1940s (Hughes, 1977, p. 94). The El Rocco also continued on without The Three Out, earning itself an international reputation, until eventually closing in 1969 (Clare & Brennan, 1995, p. 72). By that time, jazz didn't hold the same appeal to younger generations compared to its popularity over the preceding decades (Scott-Maxwell & Whiteoak, 2003, pp. 379–80).

The failure of Lee Gordon's jazz festival in 1960 had shown there wasn't as strong a demand to see jazz in concert as there was to see rock music. While rock shows filled Sydney's stadium with teenagers and caused traffic jams (The Sydney Morning Herald, 1960b), Gordon's jazz festival at the same stadium had empty seats and no traffic issues to speak of (Ford et al., 1960). Jazz was popular in Sydney, with hundreds of fans gathering to see acts organized by Freddy Logan at Jazz Club 11 (Music Maker, 1957a), or the Australian All-Stars at the Sky Lounge (Music Maker, 1960a). However, rock music had grown in popularity alongside modern jazz (Clare & Brennan, 1995, p. 83) since it arrived in Australia in 1955 (Scott-Maxwell & Whiteoak, 2003, p. 587) and would ultimately over take it.

When Lee Gordon put on a mix of American and Australian rock and roll artists in 1959 under the title of Battle of the Big Beat (Apter, 2025, p. 127), 10,000 screaming teenagers packed Sydney Stadium to see headliners Johnny O'Keefe and American Lloyd Price (The Sydney Morning Herald, 1959d). A later show in 1959 headlined by American singer Fabian was filmed by Gordon and released in cinemas as a feature length concert film *Rock'n'Roll* (1959). It shows a mostly seated audience until the end of the film when one of the performers exits the stage and is mobbed by fans as police attempt to escort them out. Fabian's performance was cut from the film so it was released featuring a lineup of Australian and New Zealand acts including Johnny O'Keefe, Johnny Rebb and Johnny Devlin (Vagg, 2023).

The Fabian concert had police struggling to control 9,000 excited teenagers (The Sydney Morning Herald, 1959e) and similar numbers, made up mostly of young teenage girls, attended Gordon's rock concerts in 1960 (The Sydney Morning Herald, 1960b). Compared to the audiences of 5,500 and 7,000 people that American jazz pianist Dave Brubeck attracted at the same venue in 1960 and 1962 respectively (K.M., 1962), it is clear tastes were changing. While rock attracted thousands of screaming teenage girls, Brubeck's audience was described as 'mainly thoughtful young men in dark suits with trimly dressed womenfolk' (K.M., 1962) who were always well behaved (L.D.H., 1960).

By 1965, the Australian jazz industry was said to have entirely collapsed. The Sky Lounge Sunday jazz sessions ended soon after, and even celebrated musicians such as Don Burrows struggled to find work (Johnson, 1987, p. 58). This was not unique to Australia. In the United States, rock 'decimated' the jazz industry during the 1960s (Anderson, 2012, p. 134), while in England, many jazz clubs were being turned into rock clubs (Male, 2021). However, modern jazz lived on at Ronnie Scott's club in London's Soho district (Forge, 2025) and we will return there in the next chapter.

Back in 1961, The Three Out's *Sittin' In* was released in December (De Looper, 2025a) and was reviewed favourably in

The Sun-Herald: 'Pianist Mike Nock plays the friendly sort of jazz you can reach out and touch on the new LP.' The newspaper went on to describe Nock as 'a master of rhythmic variations' who 'maintains a strong melody line, plating the sort of solos which linger'. It highlighted Nock and Logan's originals, 'Dizzy Pipe' and 'Nock Out', as well as Ron Falson's 'Loganberries' as songs that showed a real cohesion on the album. The review closed with a reflection on the current state of Australian jazz:

> A few years ago every Australian jazz record was in the funny
> hat Dixieland category. That's a thing of the past. This disc is
> a tribute to the maturity and idealism of our new jazzmen.
>
> (Downbeat, 1961b)

Perhaps because the trio were overseas by the time it was released, *Sittin' In* didn't receive as many reviews as *Move*. *Music Maker*, which had regularly reported on The Three Out since their formation, ended 1961 without reviewing their second album at all.

But even though The Three Out had left Australia, they were still being heard on the radio. There was, for example, a recording, likely from the Australian International Jazz Festival, aired on Australian radio in January 1962 (Australian Broadcasting Comission, 1962). *Move* was later played as part of a *Modern Songs* programme in 1963 (The Age, 1963) and the trio still appeared in playlists into the 1980s (The Sydney Morning Herald, 1987) and beyond (ABC Classic FM, 2022). However, back in 1961, The Three Out were on their way to England and their final performances together.

5   The end of The Three Out

In England, Freddy Logan once again stepped into the role of manager as he set about securing The Three Out gigs in England and Europe (Karan, 2022a). As part of this quest, he visited Paris and sat in with Americans Bud Powell and Kenny Clarke, while Nock and Karan were shown around London by the American drummer Art Taylor (Fisher & Somerville, 1961a). Nock recalled how Logan assisted The Three Out as they left Australia:

> [Freddy] knew everyone. We were immediately under contract with the Harold Davidson Agency; we worked a few gigs in England and we worked on the Continent, but I wasn't going to be there very long because I was definitely going to Berklee. No question about it, I couldn't wait to get over there.
>
> (Lewis & Lewis, 1992, p. 13)

The Three Out made their London debut at Ronnie Scott's club in July. This was reported by the English jazz magazine *Jazz News*, which noted their readers might remember Logan as 'a bassist much in demand in England a few years ago'. They added that EMI in the UK were hoping to release *Move* later that year but there was a problem (Jazz News, 1961). Chris Karan explained:

> Unfortunately, we weren't represented very well before we left [Australia] because we were hoping to do some work

in Europe and in London with the group, but the albums weren't released in England. Nobody had heard of The Three Out so we just did a few gigs.

(Karan, 2022a)

Following their introduction in London, the trio played some clubs including opposite saxophonist Tubby Hayes at the Flamingo, then visited the Netherlands before they separated (Meehan, 2010, p. 56). Logan and Karan continued as a trio with an American pianist replacing Nock (Ward, 1961). His name has since been forgotten:

> It might have been Brian Lemon. But it didn't last long because at that time I met up with Dudley [Moore] anyway and then I did three years with him.

(Karan, 2022a)

Unfortunately, the London jazz scene wasn't inviting towards outsiders at that time. Mike Nock found the local musicians cold and uninterested in talking to him. It was only when he was leaving that one of the musicians at Ronnie Scott's revealed they were only like that because they expected he'd stay and take their jobs (Meehan, 2010, p. 56). Chris Karan had a similar experience initially, later explaining that the scene was more xenophobic than it would later become:

> Musicians weren't interested in foreigners in those days. I think rock music has altered a lot of things since then and made it easier for all musicians to find work.

(Boothroyd, 1978)

Karan formed a quintet with fellow Australian saxophonist Blue Kellow, pianist Stan Jones, bassist Brian Jones and trumpeter Chris Bateson, performing together in November 1960 for the first time (Fisher & Somerville, 1961b). However, because of how unwelcome he felt, he'd begun saving money for a return ticket to Australia. He only stayed after Logan introduced him to the British musician and actor Dudley Moore (Boothroyd, 1978). In Karan's words:

> There was a club called The Establishment, run by Peter Cook, and Dudley was playing there with his trio. Freddy was playing there with another trio, and then I had this phone call from him, and he said, 'Chris, there's a guy here called Dudley Moore, and I don't think he's particularly happy with his drummer. I think it might be a good idea if you came and meet him and sit in.' And I went down there and got introduced.
>
> (Karan, 2022a)

At the time, Karan didn't know of Dudley Moore. However, he liked what he heard at the club and after their introductions Moore told him he could start the next Monday. This job offer postponed any plans of returning home to Australia and Karan remained in England (Karan, 2022a).

After Nock left for the United States, Logan had joined English saxophonist Johnny Dankworth's Dankworth All Stars (Club 43, 1961). He then rejoined the Tommy Whittle Quartet (Ward, 1961), with whom he had recorded previously in 1956. Although Logan didn't record with Whittle this time, he would be back in the studio soon when he was reunited with another musician from his previous time in England, saxophonist Tubby Hayes. By chance, in early 1962, Tubby Hayes's quartet discovered they were being paid a lot less than their bandleader and they all quit. In need of a new band, Hayes recruited trumpeter Jimmy Deuchar, pianist Gordon Beck, drummer Allan Ganley and Freddy Logan (Spillett, 2021). The new band played together in February 1962, recording a BBC session that was much later released as an LP in 2009 (Tubby Hayes Band, 2009). They then made their live debut at Ronnie Scott's club that month (Jazz News, 1962). Two later performances at Scott's in May 1962 were recorded and released on the albums *Late Spot at Scott's* (1963) and *Down in The Village* (1964) (Spillett, 2017, p. 160).

Chris Karan was among the crowds who would go to see the Tubby Hayes Quintet play at Ronnie Scott's (Karan, 2022a). Several other musicians from the Sydney jazz scene also found their way there in the coming years, including pianist Ted Nettelbeck and bassists Rick Laird and Bruce Cale (Cale, 2022). When they arrived on the London scene, Logan often assisted the Australians in finding gigs, including for Ted Nettelbeck when he arrived in 1962. Nettelbeck remembered:

> He was a lovely guy. I've realised since, I don't think he had a special interest in me at all, he was just one of those guys who loved the music and anything that he could do, that might seem to him to advance it in some way, he'd take it on. Just before I left England at the beginning of 1965, Freddy was running the music in a big hotel, and he rang me and wanted me to audition to accompany Dakota Staton, but I didn't do it because I'd already bought a ticket home. My impression was he was thinking of coming back [to Australia] in the not-too-distant future, but after that he went to work with [Dakota] Staton.
>
> (Nettelbeck, 2022)

For Logan, his time in Australia wasn't entirely forgotten. In 1966, he told Australian magazine *The Bulletin* that he preferred Australian audiences to those he played to in England: 'They were more discerning and you played better because they didn't applaud just everything' (Taylor, 1966). Logan also continued to perform his original compositions, including 'Freshwater', which he had recorded twice in Australia with The Australian All-Stars and The Three Out (Logan, 1965).

Even after Tubby Hayes disbanded his quintet in August 1964 (Jewell, 1964), Logan continued to play with Hayes until at least October 1966 (Davis & Spillett, 2015, p. 119). However, Logan felt that Hayes was moving too far into the more experimental style of free jazz of which he was not a fan (Caddy, 2022). Logan had left the group before Hayes recorded his next album *Mexican Green* (1967), where he explored his free jazz interests (Farbey, 2005).

Alongside Logan's work with Hayes, he was a member of the Stan Tracy Trio (Clayton, 1966), toured with Dakota Staton (Hennessey, 1965) and accompanied other acts at Ronnie Scott's such as Sonny Rollins (Clifton, 1966). Additionally, Logan made several appearances on BBC radio's *Jazz Club* programme with his own groups such as The Freddy Logan Afro-Cuban Big Band (BBC, 1965a) and The Freddy Logan Trio (BBC, 1965b). He also appeared on other BBC radio programmes such as *The Jazz Scene* (BBC, 1967) and BBC TV programmes such as *Jazz 625* (BBC, 1964). Although these appearances suggest someone with a busy career, Bruce Cale said after 1966 he heard about Logan less and less and thought he may have withdrawn from the jazz scene (Cale, 2022). Then, in the mid-1970s, Logan left England for America, which is when most of his London friends lost touch with him entirely.

Mike Nock

After leaving The Three Out in London, Mike Nock had arrived at Berklee College of Music near the end of 1961, only to find his scholarship wouldn't cover the cost of tuition or housing. This left Nock in 'deep shit' (Meehan, 2010, p. 61), as he recalled:

> I got to the States and realised I'm basically penniless. I could have had quite a successful career had I stayed in Australia actually, but music means something different to me. I had a vision for myself. Not to be famous, but just playing at a level that I knew was possible from all the people that I'd heard.
>
> (Nock, 2024)

Initially, Nock was able to survive by taking jobs washing dishes (Lewis & Lewis, 1992, p. 13). However, he found studying music difficult when all he wanted to do was play (Meehan, 2010, p. 64) and he contemplated moving to Canada to pursue a career there (Lewis & Lewis, 1992, p. 13). When he went to tell his professor, Nock was instead offered a job performing with a trio, allowing him to stay at school a bit longer (Meehan, 2010, p. 64). However, he dropped out after one and a half semesters when he had found enough work.

One of the clubs Nock played at was Connolly's Stardust Room in Boston. There, he spent one week supporting Yusef Lateef, who would remember Nock when he was in need of a pianist the next year (Meehan, 2010, pp. 69–70). In June 1964, Lateef hired Nock and they immediately played a series of gigs at Pep's Lounge in Philadelphia. These were recorded for Impulse Records and released across four albums between 1965 and 1978 (Meehan, 2010, pp. 72–3). After touring the country for eighteen months with Lateef (Meehan, 2010, p. 73), Nock got tired of being on the road and relocated to New York (Rozek, 1977). While there, he played in groups led by modern jazz luminaries Art Blakey, Stanley Turrentine and Booker Ervin (Rozek, 1977) and returned to the studio to lead a session for Columbia University Radio in late 1965.

At this session, alongside five of his own compositions, Nock recorded others by Ornette Coleman and Sam Rivers. They all remain unreleased, though a second session at the same studio in 1966 was eventually released a decade later (Meehan, 2010, pp. 92–3). Unlike on his recordings with The Three Out, Nock was now playing in a style he called 'free bebop' (Berg, 1978). This featured free improvisation and showed an awareness of then-current trends within jazz (Czyz, 1979).

Nock would venture further away from the sound he'd perfected in Sydney by the end of the 1960s as he embraced more electric instrumentation (Meehan, 2010, pp. 126, 132). This begun in 1968 when Nock was a member of the John Handy Concert Ensemble, which also featured Mike White, one of the few jazz violinists (Wilson, 1968). On the side, Nock and White formed The Mike Nock Quartet, which was made up of John Handy's band without Handy. Nock continued playing in both bands until he found out they were being underpaid compared to Handy and he and White quit (Meehan, 2010, p. 118).

Their work with Handy was notable for how it fused jazz and rock. They continued with that sound when they formed their next group (The San Francisco Examiner, 1968). Initially billed as The Fourth Wave, the group made their debut at San Francisco's Jazz Workshop in August 1968 (The San Francisco Examiner, 1968). The name had changed to The Fourth Way by September and a second performance at the Jazz Workshop was described as 'a most profound experience' by *The San Francisco Examiner* (Elwood, 1968).

It was during this period that Nock switched to electric piano and The Fourth Way released three albums of electric jazz between 1968 and 1970. Their third was recorded live at

Switzerland's Montreux Jazz Festival in June 1970 (Meehan, 2010, pp. 125, 161–2). Following their appearance at the festival, they travelled to Germany, where Nock was to record an album for MPS Records. The session was recorded as a trio, with members of the Fourth Way bassist Ron McClure and percussionist Eddie Marshall accompanying Nock. Only White was missing from the lineup (Meehan, 2010, p. 154). White was offended at being left out, and although the Fourth Way continued on their European tour following the session, they ultimately broke up in 1971 (Meehan, 2010, pp. 154, 161–2).

The album Nock recorded for MPS was released as *Between or Beyond* in 1971 credited to The Mike Nock Underground (Hi Fi Stereophonie, 1971). This was Nock's first album released with him as leader. It would then be several more years before another Nock lead album appeared in 1977. This was when the aforementioned session recorded in 1966 at Columbia University was released as *Almanac* (Meehan, 2010, pp. 92–3). Over the next five years, Nock was extremely prolific as a leader, releasing seven albums including the widely praised *Ondas*, recorded in 1981 (Meehan, 2010, pp. 238–9, 296–7).

Nock returned to Australia in 1985, accepting a three-month residency at the Brisbane Conservatorium of Music. This was subsequently extended to a year. While there, Nock received a call from Don Burrows offering him an opportunity to teach at the Sydney Conservatorium (Meehan, 2010, pp. 252–6). Nock accepted and remained in the position until 2018 (Promethean Editions, 2024).

The El Rocco jazz club also returned, re-opening in 1987 with Nock taking a Sunday residency (Hessey, 1987). This was followed by a documentary film, *Beyond El Rocco*, released in 1990 which celebrated the club and the surrounding jazz scene. Nock was among those featured and the film includes interviews and a performance from him. The Three Out's album *Move* appears on screen briefly while Nock discusses doing 'a number of illicit things which we won't go into' that were part of the scene at the time. The Three Out are otherwise left unmentioned (Beyond El Rocco, 1990). The same thing happened when a documentary on Nock aired in Australia in 1994. There was surprise the film skipped over his early success in Sydney. Gail Brennan wrote in *The Sydney Morning Herald*:

> Mike Nock did not, as this New Zealand doco implies, go straight from remote Narawokia [*sic*] to the big time in New York. First he came to Australia, where he played in Johnny O'Keefe's band and took his own brilliant trio into the Kings Cross jazz club El Rocco.

(Brennan, 1994)

Nock has since been immortalised in the far more comprehensive biography *Serious Fun: The Life and Music of Mike Nock*, published in 2010. This details his career across New Zealand, Australia, the United States and back to Australia, up to its publication.

Since then, Nock has remained incredibly productive within the Australian jazz scene. This is something he said was ultimately thanks to The Three Out:

> There was always a buzz around The Three Out. For some reason or other, we were the cats, and when I came back, I had something to come back to. Because, when you do stuff at a certain period in your life it reverberates. It really does. And what happened to me was, people kept bringing me back.

(Nock, 2024)

Chris Karan

While Freddy Logan worked with Tubby Hayes, and Mike Nock toured America, Chris Karan had joined the Dudley Moore Trio in 1961. He also found work as a session musician, though he often didn't know what the recordings were for until after they'd been released. This was the case when he worked on French singer Serge Gainsbourg's 1973 album *Vu De L'Extérieur* as well as sessions with Jimmy Page, David Bowie and Bob Marley (Karan, 2022b):

> I did a lot of these recordings, but we never knew who they were for. I'd never heard of these names, because we used to do the backing tracks and then all these artists used to come in and overdub their voices. We'd do the tracks, pack up, and go to the next session. We didn't meet the artists.
>
> (Karan, 2022b)

Beginning in the late 1960s, Karan also recorded several sessions with Roy Budd, including his first album *Pick Yourself Up*, released in 1967. In addition, he also worked on film soundtracks with Budd such as *Get Carter* (Discogs, 2025d):

> Roy did about 40 scores, and I virtually did all of them with him. There's a very nice one called *Diamonds*. It's one of Roy's nicest, and I'm on there ticking away.
>
> (Karan, 2025)

Karan's work with the Dudley Moore Trio also included film work. This included their appearance in *30 Is a Dangerous Age, Cynthia* (30 Is a Dangerous Age, Cynthia, 1968) and their soundtrack to Moore's 1967 film *Bedazzled* (Paskin, 2000, p. 432). The trio's first album together, *Dudley Moore Plays the Theme from Beyond the Fringe & All That Jazz*, had been released in 1962 credited solely to Moore (Moore, 1962). It wasn't until 1965 that their first album credited as The Dudley Moore Trio was released. That album, *The Other Side of Dudley Moore*, became the best-selling jazz album in Britain at the time (Paskin, 2000, p. 94). It was followed by *Genuine Dud* in 1966 (Paskin, 2000, p. 94) and a self-titled album *The Dudley Moore Trio* in 1969. Moore was highly complementary of Karan's playing as a member of his trio:

> Chris is a fantastic timekeeper. In fact, for my money he's one of the best timekeepers I know. He doesn't do a great deal of fooling about and filling in. But there's a crispness to his playing, plus the actual rhythmic instinct and sensitivity to the beat that he has. It's not only a good, solid beat, but also it's one that's buoyant.
>
> (Tomkins, 1966)

The Dudley Moore Trio toured Australia several times. This allowed Karan to see his family again (Karan, 2025). The local press reminded their readers of The Three Out, describing Karan as the Australian drummer who 'played in the Three Out Trio with Freddy Logan and New Zealand pianist Mike Nock in Sydney before it split' (Foster, 1971). Following their 1978 tour of Australia, Moore shifted his focus onto his acting career and his trio went on indefinite hiatus. A recording of the Australian tour became their final album together, *Dudley Down Under*, and it would be over a decade before they shared a stage again, eventually reuniting in 1992 (Paskin, 2000, pp. 162–3, 329, 433).

During the 1970s, Karan continued his session work. He enjoyed this as it brought him into regular contact with other players from whom he was able to learn new techniques and share ideas to improve his playing (Boothroyd, 1978). He also became known as one of the few in England who had mastered instruments such as the tabla, darbuka, berimbau, cuica, bongo, timbales and conga, with Karan creating his own congas as a side business (Boothroyd, 1978):

> I got interested in producing my own conga drums, and I made some cuica, which are a Brazilian drum, and cabasa. Percussionist used to call me up because I was making a few things that they didn't know about, and I sold quite a few of them. It was kind of a hobby that I enjoyed doing.
>
> (Karan, 2025)

Alongside his session work, Karan made regular appearances on TV programmes in England (Karan, 2025). These included talk show *Parkinson* as part of The Harry Stoneham Big Band. Karan explained:

> I used to meet up with Harry on sessions and he said he'd been invited to do a chat show with Micheal Parkinson, and would I like to do it? So, we got together and also did some trio things with Pete Morgan on bass. I did the show for about eight years, and then they continued with a new band and new concept. I did a lot of television because it was the days when everybody had their own show, so there was always something to do. I had a Brazilian group called Sugarloaf, and did projects for the BBC for about four years. Just broadcasts, we never performed live, but that was enjoyable.
>
> (Karan, 2025)

After his time with Harry Stoneham came to an end, Karan spent the next several decades with flamenco guitarist Juan Martin, touring together into the 2010s with a band mixing Latin jazz and flamenco sounds. Karan has since retired from music (Karan, 2025). However, his past recordings continue to be heard, with albums from Roy Budd and the Dudley Moore Trio reissued alongside Karan's appearances in the many studio sessions he took part in.

Freddy Logan

In 1974, Freddy Logan had relocated to the United States. He spent some time in Los Angeles, where he found the jazz community unwelcoming and later expressed regret that he hadn't gone to New York (Caddy, 2023). Instead, he found work as band leader onboard MS *Nordic Prince* (Myers, 1974).

After placing an advertisement in English magazine *Melody Maker* for a singer to join his band, Logan received a letter from Catherine Kelly and Logan replied that he would be in London at the beginning of 1976 to make the final arrangements. Kelly didn't take up his offer; however, they would stay in touch. By 1981, Logan had returned to London and was living with Kelly in Kensington Gardens. The two married in 1983 and welcomed a son Ryan the following year (Caddy, 2023). Logan, meanwhile, found work leading bands at The New Bogart's restaurant (The New Bogart's, 1981) and later the Sheraton Skyline at Heathrow Airport in their Colony Room (Heppie, 1983).

Pianist Nick Weldon performed with Logan's band through the 1980s, which he described as 'a commercial band with residencies in various places – getting worse year by year'. Some of their locations included 'the Empress in Mayfair, then the Hilton in Park Lane, and finally in a Chinese restaurant in Queensway!' (Weldon, 2023)

By then, as several of his bandmates recalled, Logan had developed a complicated relationship with his past work. Weldon said Logan didn't like to talk about his past, explaining: 'I think he was quite bitter about the way it had worked out for him – and he seemed to enjoy getting keen young jazz pianists into his commercial band and giving them a hard time' (Weldon, 2023). Weldon's first experience with Logan led him to quit after a few weeks though he returned to sit-in with the band through the 1980s. He found Logan provided valuable lessons to him alongside his scorn (Weldon, 2023). Pianist Simon Wallace played with Logan's band at The Hilton and Sheraton Skyline and was able to speak with Logan about his jazz past, even if the topic remained complicated:

> When I knew him, he certainly hadn't lost interest in music but was adamant that he didn't want to be part of the jazz scene again. I did manage to drag him down to Ronnie [Scott]'s one night but despite being treated like the returning prodigal son by Ronnie and Pete [King, co-founder of Ronnie Scott's jazz club] that night, I don't think he ever went back there. Fred was a somewhat complicated man … very often not easy to get on with.
>
> (Wallace, 2023)

Unfortunately, after injuring his hand in a car accident, Logan was forced to leave music behind and worked as a taxi driver until his retirement (Caddy, 2023). Although he later spent some time looking back through his career and compiling old recordings, Logan rarely did interviews and never wrote an account of his life in jazz. This has left him less well known than many of his contemporaries.

'Fred was a very modest and discreet person', Logan's brother-in-law Brian Caddy said. 'When I asked him if he had ever considered writing a book about his career, he said he would never tell tales about his fellow musicians.' Instead, he shared with Caddy that his favourite bass players were Ron

Carter, Niels-Henning Ørsted Pedersen, Scott La Faro and Charlie Haden. His favourite music was 1970s Brazilian jazz fusion and his favourite album was George Duke's *Brazilian Love Affair* (1980) (Caddy, 2022).

Freddy Logan appeared on over forty releases across his jazz career, but didn't keep many of his recordings. Both of The Three Out albums were an exception, alongside his first two albums with Tubby Hayes, and Kenny Clare and Ronnie Stephenson's *Drum Spectacular* (1966). Following a long battle with cancer, Freddy Logan died 3 May 2003 aged 73 (Caddy, 2023).

Out, But Not Forgotten

Each member of The Three Out found further success after leaving Australia in 1961. Yet, *Move* remained an important work within each of their careers. It is of course one of the earliest albums in each of their discographies. However, it also showed off their already developed skills as musicians and composers.

Freddy Logan had already made several recordings with successful groups in England and the Netherlands. Though it was only in Australia that he began recording his own compositions. On *Move*, Logan's skill shines through on his two originals as does his playing throughout the album. While he later found greater international recognition during his time with Tubby Hayes, Logan's own compositions appear on none of these albums. His time with The Three Out is important then as a record of his ability and creativity as a composer which otherwise went largely unheard.

Alongside Logan, Chris Karan and Mike Nock shared credit on 'Way Back'. It was the only song on *Move* credited to all three members and was the first-time compositions by Karan and Nock had appeared on a record. While Karan's later session work saw him largely uncredited throughout his career the number of compositions by Nock would only grow. *Move* was the beginning.

The success of *Move* further showed that The Three Out weren't just popular amongst the small group of hipsters who could fill the El Rocco jazz club in Sydney. They were popular across Australia. It was a pivotal moment where they could have stayed in Australia to hold onto their place as Sydney's best-known modern jazz trio. However, their popularity gave them the confidence to attempt to make it overseas. They left behind a strong reputation as well as two albums.

Because their second album *Sittin' In* was released after The Three Out had already left Australia, *Move* is the one that cemented The Three Out's place in Australian jazz history. *Move* is a time capsule for the modern jazz heard in Sydney's El Rocco basement where The Three Out performed almost every night. It stands as an example of the strengths of a local jazz scene featuring some of the highest celebrated musicians of the time. Few others were recorded. So, alongside albums by The Australian All Stars and The Bryce Rohde Quartet, *Move* is a lasting example of Australian modern jazz at the beginning of the 1960s. Further to this, when Mike Nock and Chris Karan later returned to Australia they did so with an existing reputation. Because people remembered The Three Out and, importantly, they remembered *Move*. The strength of their work in 1960 has meant we are still talking about *Move* today.

6 *Move*: An annotated bibliography and discography

Although all three of The Three Out members had left Australia in 1961, both Chris Karan and Mike Nock returned several times to perform with their respective groups and the press made sure to remind their readers of their prior local success. While on tour with Dudley Moore in the 1970s, Karan was described as 'a well-known figure on the local jazz scene in the late fifties' (Jackson, 1978) who played in The Three Out before they split (Foster, 1971). While Adrian Jackson wrote of Nock: 'Whenever people recall the good old days of jazz in Australia in the '50s, they always mention pianist Mike Nock and his funk jazz trio The Three Out' (Jackson, 1979). The reminiscences continued into the 1980s when Eric Myers recalled The Three Out as 'the top jazz group in the country' who had released *Move*, 'one of the classic albums of Australian jazz history' (Myers, 1981). Adrian Jackson again reminded his readers of the 'very influential' Three Out when Nock returned in 1984 (Jackson, 1984), and Gail Brennan recalled 'the famous Three Out Trio, which was the most popular band in the early days of the El Rocco' when profiling Nock in 1988 (Brennan, 1988).

These mentions were all in Australian newspapers, however, beginning in the 1970s, The Three Out were also referenced in several books published on Australian jazz history. One of the earliest books on Australian jazz (Williams, 1981, p. 41), *Daddy's*

Practising Again: An Australian Jazzman Looks Back and Around by Dick Hughes was published in 1977 and briefly mentions The Three Out: 'It was a good year for jazz in Sydney, 1961. The Three Out, consisting of Mike Nock (piano), Freddie Logan (bass), Chris Karen (drums) had enlivened the early months of the year at El Rocco.' Elsewhere, he recalls Nock playing a grand piano at the El Rocco (Hughes, 1977, pp. 83–4, 93).

Two years later *Black Roots, White Flowers: A History of Jazz in Australia* by Andrew Bisset was published in 1979, then revised in 1987. The Three Out are mentioned, though unfortunately both editions contain a major error in claiming Freddy Logan joined The Embers band in Melbourne with Mike Nock and Chris Karan (Bisset, 1987, p. 108). They fared better in Bruce Johnson's *The Oxford Companion to Australian Jazz* (1987) where The Three Out's career is summarized in an entry about the El Rocco jazz club. Although he doesn't mention their albums, Johnson details the trio's work at the El Rocco, Pigalle and Primatif clubs as well as their inclusion in Lee Gordon's jazz festival and their New Zealand tour (Johnson, 1987, pp. 148–9).

Move is pictured in John Clare's *Bodgie Dada & the Cult of Cool: Australian Jazz Since 1945* (1995), illustrating an early chapter about the El Rocco. The Three Out are mentioned some ten pages later and Nock is quoted describing their audience and the sensation The Three Out caused inside the small club where they formed, though the year is listed as 1959 rather than in 1960 (Clare & Brennan, 1995, pp. 56, 68–9). The book includes further mentions of the trio (Clare & Brennan, 1995, pp. 95–6, 116), and was accompanied by a CD compilation and television documentary which both included Mike Nock. I have not been able to view the latter and I will mention the CD again shortly.

Mike Nock was the subject of Norman Meehan's *Serious Fun: The Life and Music of Mike Nock* (2010) which includes a chapter on The Three Out (Meehan, 2010, pp. 46–57). He was also the subject of chapters in John Sharpe's *I wanted to be a Jazz Musician* (2008) and John Shand's *Jazz: The Australian Accent* (2009). Sharpe called The Three Out 'well respected but unfortunately short lived' and in his interview with Nock they discuss the trio's time in Sydney before moving on to his career in America (Sharpe, 2008, pp. 137–54). Shand's interview with Nock is more focused on his return to Australia in the 1980s than his early years, though The Three Out do receive a quick mention (Shand, 2009, p. 47). More recently, Andrew Robson's *Austral jazz: the localization of a global music form in Sydney* (2020) contained a section titled 'Mike Nock and The 3 Out Trio'. This summarized the trio's career with a strong focus on Nock. Both The Three Out albums are described and there is some analysis of *Sittin' In* (Robson, 2021, pp. 33–5).

While the above indicates The Three Out were important enough in Australian jazz history to be mentioned, their music remained largely unavailable outside of the second-hand market. There had been two vinyl pressings of *Move* in both mono and stereo. The first released in 1961 (3-Out, 1961), and a second as part of Columbia's Encore Series released sometime between 1964 and 1983 (De Looper, 2025b). It's likely the repress was released during the 1960s, as The Australian All-Stars album *Jazz For Beach-Niks* was also included in the series in 1968 (Wes, 1968). However, an exact date for the reissue of *Move* is unclear.

Those unable to find a copy of *Move* could finally hear one song from the album in 1995 when 'Way Back' was included on the CD compilation *Bodgie Dada & The Cult of*

Cool, a companion to the book of the same name which documented the history of Australian jazz. Unfortunately, the song was miscredited to The Mike Nock Trio (Various, 1995).

The following year, 'Little Niles' was included on another CD compilation, *History of Jazz In Australia*, correctly credited to The Three Out (The University of Melbourne, 2006). This project had originated with a plan to release a set of albums to commemorate Australia's Bicentenary in 1988, but evolved into a collection of compilations on Australian music history (Miliano, 2012, pp. 23, 26). For the jazz compilation, former EMI producer Ron Wills collected forty songs recorded between 1925 and 1989 across two CDs (The University of Melbourne, 2006). While many of the other included songs and artists had previously appeared elsewhere, it was the first time 'Little Niles' had appeared anywhere besides on *Move*.

Later in 2015, the Australian Jazz Museum released their own double CD compilation of Australian modern jazz titled *The Cool School of the 1950s*, which included The Three Out's 'Way Back' (Australian Jazz Museum, 2015). Needless to say, both Three Out albums were long out of print by the 2000s, even as they remained a reference point when discussing Mike Nock's work within Australian jazz (Sutherland, 2008). *Move* in particular had become highly sought after by collectors, with Votary Records's James Pianta listing *Move* at number two in his Top Ten Rare Australian Jazz Records, writing it was: 'One of the holy grails of Australian Jazz records. This revered recording is sublime Australian Modern Jazz' (Egan, 2008). In Japan, Mike Nock had seen a copy of *Move* on sale for US$3,000 in the early 2000s being sold by the Japanese jazz record label DIW. The label asked Nock if he could find more copies. They hoped to do a reissue to capitalize on how much people were willing to pay for an original, but it didn't happen (Kee, 2016).

Among collectors, both albums from The Three Out had also been selling on online marketplaces for high prices. A copy of *Sittin In'* sold on eBay for over A$100 in 2008 (Value Your Music, 2008), while a copy of *Move* sold for over A$500 in 2009 (Value Your Music, 2009). Although they had only been sold in Australia upon release, clearly several copies had made their way overseas as many of those being sold online were being sold from the UK, Europe and United States (Discogs, 2024). The Italian DJ and Blue Note Records artist Nicola Conte discovered a copy of *Move* in 2004, as he told *Now Toronto* at the time:

> One of my recent finds. It's a top early-60s Australian jazz piano trio session involving Mike Nock, Freddie Logan and Chris Karan. It's got a deep version of Randy Weston's Little Niles and a great Afro-modal tune called Primitive.

> (Conte, 2004)

It's not clear why The Three Out remained unavailable on CD or digitally, but much of the early Australian modern jazz from this period has also remained unavailable on modern formats. Previously discussed examples of recordings by Pat Caplice, The Music Maker All Stars and even Don Burrows have also remained unavailable outside their original vinyl releases. While some recordings from this era have been collected by the Australian Jazz Museum (Australian Jazz Museum, 2015), and others like the Russ Arno album featuring Freddy Logan were reissued on CD by specialist label Lyric (Arno, 2002), few have made the jump to streaming services like *Spotify*. There is one noteworthy exception. Both albums from The Australian

All-Stars were remastered and reissued on CD in Japan by Solid Records in 2013 (Disk Union, n.d.), and are currently available on streaming services worldwide (Spotify, n.d.). Similarly, it would take someone outside of Australia to bring The Three Out back too.

7   *Move* reissued

In 2015, both albums by The Three Out were reissued by German record label Be! Jazz. The label had been reissuing obscure and largely forgotten jazz albums for several years, and when a friend of label owner Micha Gottschalk was visiting Australia, Gottschalk asked him to find some Australian jazz albums. Amongst those he received were the two Three Out albums, and he decided to reissue them both (Gottschalk, 2025).

Although part of the original *Move* master tape exists and is held by the National Film and Sound Archive of Australia (National Film and Sound Archive of Australia, 1960), the remasters released by Gottschalk were made from a recording of the 1961 vinyl release. Gottschalk had contacted EMI in Germany, asking if they had any of The Three Out master tapes. He was told they had no record of the albums at all. Consequently, he had to rely on making a vinyl transfer for both albums (Gottschalk, 2025). To remaster the albums, Gottschalk used Railroad Tracks, a music studio in Buir, west of Cologne, Germany. This had been founded by John Cremer after he left EMI Germany. Thomas Ölscher of Railroad Tracks recalled they had a tight budget for The Three Out project but there wasn't a lot that needed to be done outside of some de-crackle to remove any sound of the vinyl that was present on the recording (Ölscher, 2024).

The Be! Jazz reissues were limited to 500 units of each vinyl album (Be! Records, 2016a), and were pressed by Pallas using the Direct Metal Mastering technique which creates a higher quality audio during the vinyl pressing process. For the reissues, all of the original artwork was restored along with their liner notes to emulate the original pressings. The only major difference was the inclusion of the Be! Records logo and credits for the remaster (Be! Records, 2016b).

For the CD release, they were packaged in a digipack paper case with a small booklet reproducing the liner notes next to photos from the original vinyl sleeve. The booklet also included additional advertisements for other releases from Be! Jazz (3-Out, 2015). Once released, copies were exported to Japan, the United States and Australia for sale (Kee, 2016). Although neither Mike Nock nor Chris Karan was involved, they were happy to have them made available again. Nock has remarked:

> Most of my records get released on CD and usually I'm the
> last person to know … I'm not one of those jazz musicians
> that's in it for the money, so I'm happy that the music gets
> out there and has legs.
>
> (Presley, 2016)

Karan later added:

> It's nice they put those out on CD. I enjoyed doing those
> albums, particularly at a young age. I mean I was only 19 or
> 20 then, and it was great fun.
>
> (Karan, 2022a)

While the reissues meant both Three Out albums were now more widely available on vinyl and CD, the price for original vinyl pressings has remained high. A copy of the Columbia reissue of *Move* sold for A\$270 in 2020 (Value Your Music, 2020), while a near mint 1961 first pressing of *Move* sold for £225 (A\$427.68) in 2022 (Discogs, 2024). Even the trio's second album *Sittin' In* sold for A\$639 in 2016 (Value Your Music, 2016), suggesting the repress from Be! Records did nothing to lower prices of the originals.

But for those uninterested in paying hundreds of dollars for an original, the reissues from Be! Records were welcomed. The Australian journalist John Shand considered the two reissues to be part of a 'major retrospective of Oz jazz', alongside other recent reissues at the time. Shand, though, was surprised that 'an obscure German label has re-released some pivotal albums from this era of Australian jazz'. Of *Move*, he wrote:

> While Nock's playing was not quite as distinctive as it is now, it already contained the ebullience that remains such a prominent feature of his work … Any fan of the modern-day Nock should hear this.
>
> (Shand, 2016)

At the end of 2016, Sydney record store Birdland listed their top albums of the year, with The Three Out's *Move* taking the first position of Australian acts (Wilson, 2017). Other record stores also had high praise for The Three Out, with American store Dusty Groove reviewing both albums. They praised the trio's work on *Move*, writing they 'really know how to make the record groove – especially in comparison to other Aussie jazz dates from the time' (Dusty Groove, Inc., n.d.a). For *Sittin 'In*, they highlighted Freddy Logan, 'whose sound gives the record this deep bottom right from the start, and puts the group on a par with a rare few American trios – like the Three Sounds on Blue Note!' They further praised the inclusion of a horn section on the album's B-Side, which they felt made it even more interesting (Dusty Groove, Inc., n.d.b).

Move Live

To celebrate the reissue, Mike Nock discussed reforming The Three Out along with Chris Karan and a new bassist but at the last minute it didn't happen (Nock, 2022). Instead, Nock took his Mike Nock Trio out to perform a series of shows billed as The Three Out Redux, revisiting the *Move* album with bassist Brett Hirst and drummer James Waples (The Australian Music Centre, 2016).

This trio had been together in different forms for close to a decade when they performed the Redux shows. Though the trio had previously featured Tony Hall on drums and James Waples's brother Ben on bass (Nock, 2004), James Waples and Hirst took over around the time that Nock decided to do The Three Out Redux shows. James Waples explained:

> Mike just kind of sprung it upon us. When we played The Three Out stuff, I learnt it from playing with Mike and then I went home to check out the album. But in a way, I didn't want to go and copy it, and Mike would have killed me if I did that anyway. He wouldn't want me to play what Chris Karan played. We didn't play all of the tracks, and maybe picked four or five. It wasn't a big thing, and I don't think Mike intended it to be a reunion tour of the album, it was more like the album was being re-released so we played a couple of songs. Because back then, you had to go to the library to find it, unless someone put it on *YouTube* or something.
>
> (Waples, 2024)

The Redux show debuted 4 December 2015 at Foundry616 in Sydney (Nock, 2015) and returned 12 February 2016 (The Australian Music Centre, 2016), before moving to Melbourne's

Bird's Basement on 30 March (Bird's Basement, 2016) and Brisbane's QPAC Cremorne Theatre 1 April (Sutton, 2016). It was then revived 3 December 2019 at Smith's Alternative in Canberra (Smith's Alternative, 2019).

Ahead of the second Sydney show, Nock took to Facebook to share that they would be mixing new material alongside that from *Move*, and wrote, 'I'm reminded of how good this music was and keep finding more and more contemporary relevance in it' (Nock, 2016a). Afterwards he added:

> Back in 1960, if anyone had suggested that in 2016, I'd be doing a gig in Sydney, playing music from my then new recording, MOVE, I would have thought they were seriously deranged. But here I am.
>
> (Nock, 2016b)

With only a handful of Redux shows held, it's unfortunate that few reviews or recordings exist to properly document them as at the time Nock talked encouragingly about how the shows would revisit the 1960 material:

> We're learning the original arrangements as a starting point to play the music from our current perspective of 55 years later. This is turning out to be a bigger challenge than I originally thought, but I'm finding it an incredibly interesting process and a huge journey of self-discovery, as the music contains most of the concepts I've spent my lifetime exploring ever since.
>
> (Kee, 2016)

Geoff Page organized the 2019 Redux show in Canberra as part of his regular Geoff's Jazz series of events held at Smith's Alternative. He had seen The Three Out perform at El Rocco in 1960 and enjoyed their album *Move*, so he was happy Nock agreed to bring back his Redux show after the last held in 2016 (Page, 2025).

> I often like to get musicians to go back to their roots. A lot don't want to and are reluctant to play great jazz compositions they learned in school, so I was pleasantly surprised Mike was prepared to do a revisit gig of Three Out songs for my series, as I understood he had disowned some of his early work. The gig itself was a pretty loose interpretation of the original 45-minute LP, and there were a few things that certainly weren't on the original record. I thought he had to labour somewhat on the Smith's rather worn out upright, but the energy came through. It certainly was a night to remember, and I remember mainly energy and good humour.
>
> (Page, 2025)

The trio performed two sets. They opened the first with 'Squeeze Me', though it was played at a much slower pace than how it had appeared on *Move*. This was followed by 'Lollipops and Roses', a song Nock said he'd played in the United States during the 1960s. 'Now it's not a Three Out song', Nock explained. 'But, hey, we're going to be playing some songs that are kind of from the era, kind of in a loose way. This is jazz after all and it's about making some interesting music' (Nock, 2019). Later, the trio performed Art Blakey & The Messengers's 'Moanin'. Nock explained this wasn't on The Three Out album either but was a composition they played back then. After a break, they returned to play a second set and Nock introduced another song from *Move*:

> We're going to hear a piece that hasn't been heard in a long time. It's a piece from the first record called 'Freshwater', and

written by the wonderful bass player who has since passed, Freddy Logan. Who was actually the reason why the whole Three Out trio came about. He was our manager, inspiration, everything.

(Nock, 2019)

A set list displayed on Nock's piano during the performance featured five songs from *Move*, though only two made it into the actual performance. 'Primitive', 'Softly As In A Morning Sunrise', and 'If I Were A Bell' were not performed on the night (Pozza, 2019). A recording of the performance was later broadcast on ArtSound FM 92.7 in April 2025. It had been recorded by Smith's Alternative's sound engineer Bevan Noble, then mastered and presented by Chris Deacon for his program *Friday Night Live* (ArtSound FM 92.7, 2025).

Since 2019, the Redux shows haven't been repeated live, and The Three Out arrangements haven't reappeared in any of the Mike Nock Trio's shows either. James Warples said Nock wasn't someone who liked to look back and during the many years they had played together, Warples often suggested playing songs from Nock's *Ondas* album, but he always refused instead preferring to focus on his new work (Waples, 2024). Warples said:

> There was an attitude where he didn't want to go back and play that stuff, even though it was a success. He was like, 'I'm not going to play that, I'm writing new music.' So, I suppose it was the same with the Three Out stuff, and why we never touched it before then, and since.

(Waples, 2024)

8 Moving on

As of 2025, both *Move* and *Sittin' In* have fallen back out of print. Copies of the original vinyl pressings remain available at prices high and low, depending on the quality, while the Be! Records reissues are available as a far more affordable option. These were only reissued on CD and vinyl with Be! Records's Micha Gottschalk having no interest in a digital release. He explained that his label barely made a profit on their physical releases and would make even less from streaming services or by offering a download (Gottschalk, 2025).

One track did appear for sale digitally in 2023 as part of *A Night at Smokey Mokes*, a digital reissue of the 1996 compilation *History of Australian Jazz*, which featured 'Little Niles'. Earlier in 2022, both albums by The Three Out were also uploaded to YouTube, followed by a recording of their appearance at the First Annual Australian International Jazz Festival. *Move* has accumulated over 13,000 views since then, while *Sittin' In* has over 700 views, and the festival recording has over 400. These were each shared by the YouTube channel Music for Your Ears (YouTube, 2025), rather than any official affiliation with a record label. They remain unavailable for sale digitally.

While those stats suggest there's some interest in these albums, it seems unlikely they will be officially reissued again, and for his part, Micha Gottschalk of Be! Records felt it was unlikely to ever have happened unless he had stepped in. 'They had 50 years to do it, and when I contacted EMI they didn't even know the albums existed. So, if I hadn't released them then no one would', he said (Gottschalk, 2025).

Both of The Three Out albums have been recognized as important recordings of Australian jazz mostly because of their connection to Mike Nock as he was establishing his reputation in the first phase of a long career (Robson, 2021, pp. 33, 35). They also serve as reminders of the early history of modern jazz in Australia, before its further development during the 1970s and later. Additionally, they give insight into the musicians and their idea of jazz at the time. As Peter Rechniewski wrote in 1983, 'making a jazz record in Australia is not directly a way of making money for the musician. It is, unless you happen to be Don Burrows or John Sangster, an event of artistic documentation and as such its significance is that much greater' (Rechniewski, 1983).

Move was undoubtedly an important step in the careers of all three members of The Three Out. It featured the first recorded composition by Mike Nock, the second studio recording by Chris Karan, and has some of the few of Freddy Logan's compositions to be released. The album remains a great example of early 1960s Australian modern jazz when the 12″ album format was still new. However, the difficulty in finding copies of *Move* following its initial release had left it largely unheard before its reissue in 2015. This scarcity left it without the wider recognition I believe it deserves, outside of the most devoted jazz fans.

Since The Three Out albums were reissued, both Mike Nock and Chris Karan have once again moved on to other things. Karan has enjoyed his retirement for many years (Karan, 2025), while Nock said in 2024 he thought he might retire soon too because although people still want to see him perform, and many still want a chance to perform with him, he no longer felt he was able to perform at the standard he wanted from himself (Nock, 2024). Looking back at his time in The Three Out, Nock said:

> It was amazing! Maybe we were just lucky, but there was always a buzz around The Three Out. For some reason or other, we were the cats. It really made a huge difference in my life. It gave me the confidence to do things, because I had the top band in Australia, and I've been fortunate that Freddy took me under his wing, and Freddy being the way he was, once you start getting a few little things happening, they go your way.
>
> (Nock, 2024)

For Chris Karan, he was glad to see his early work gain recognition again following the Be! Records reissues, but remains disappointed that none of their television appearances were preserved:

> Unfortunately, we never recorded anything with The Three Out video-wise. All that time spent at the El Rocco, nobody ever bothered to film us or anything, which is really unfortunate. Even the jazz festival that we played at for Lee Gordon, that wasn't ever filmed. So, there's nothing of us for anybody to see, just two albums. I thought that was a shame, as it was such a nice trio and we all got on very well.
>
> (Karan, 2022a)

Reflecting on the matter again in 2025, Karan added:

> Still, it was nice how we were able to do a couple of recordings, because it's the kind of thing that didn't happen much in the early '60s. People weren't doing a lot of recording of Australian jazz.
>
> (Karan, 2025)

Likewise, after decades of not thinking highly of his performance on *Move* (Nock, 2022), Nock's opinion had warmed slightly when we spoke in 2024, though he remained his own harshest critic:

> When I listen to that first record, I'm amazed at how well I did play while I really couldn't play. It's quite bizarre. It's all about intention, and confidence. And when we did The Three Out record, I really didn't know shit. Even with the things that I think are really bad, you hear it, and there's still some talent. There's something going on there that transcends all that.
>
> (Nock, 2024)

Bibliography

30 Is a Dangerous Age, Cynthia, 1968. [Film] Directed by Joseph McGrath. England: Walter Shenson Productions.

3-Out, T., 1961. *Move* [Sound Recording] (Columbia).

3-Out, T., 2015. *Move* [Sound Recording] (Be! Jazz).

3-Out, T., n.d. *Move* [Sound Recording] (Columbia).

A.W.L., 1960. The Australian All Stars. *Jazz Notes* (104), p. 30.

ABC Classic FM, 2022. *Jazztrack Online: 10 April 2002* [Online] Available at: https://webarchive.nla.gov.au/awa/20030102014719/http://www.abc.net.au/classic/jazztrack/online_stories/s528130.htm [Accessed 22 July 2025].

ABC Weekly, 1957. Look Who's Dropped In. *ABC Weekly*, 14 August, p. 37.

Alaronde, 1955. Jazz on Records. *The Glamorgan Gazette*, 25 February, p. 9.

All-Stars, T. A., 1960. *Jazz For Beach-Niks Volume 2* [Sound Recording] (Columbia).

Amsterdam City Archives, n.d. *Archiefkaarten* [Online] Available at: https://archief.amsterdam/indexen/deeds/985333f2-2b06-56a3-e053-b784100ade19?person=985333f2-2b07-56a3-e053-b784100ade19 [Accessed 21 July 2025].

Ancestry, 1956. *UK and Ireland, Outward Passenger Lists, 1890–1960*. s.l.: National Archives, London, England.

Anderson, I., 2012. *This Is Our Music: Free Jazz, the Sixties, and American Culture*. Pennsylvania: University of Pennsylvania Press.

Anon., 1958. *Top Jazz Players Team for New A.B.C. Series*. s.l.: National Archives of Australia.

Apter, J., 2025. *Lee Gordon Presents … .* ebook ed. Summer Hill, New South Wales: Echo.

Apter, J. & Hill, S., 2025. *Meet the Man Who Brought America's Big Stars to Australia in the 1950s* [Online] Available at: https://www.abc.net.au/listen/programs/nightlife/jeff-apter-on-lee-gordon/105498760 [Accessed 12 August 2025].

Archives, A., 2022. *Email Regarding 1960 International Jazz Festival* [Interview] (29 March 2022).

Arno, R., 2002. *Russ Arno Sings* [Sound Recording] (Lyric).

ArtSound FM 92.7, 2025. *Facebook ArtSound FM 92.7* [Online] Available at: https://www.facebook.com/artsoundfm/posts/pfbid02m6RrgWU83R3yFkKwWQgKRUjNBAhK5Anmg3N9QugW65ut4M7PkERDVRLrGyXsnSnLl [Accessed 26 July 2025].

Australian Broadcasting Commission, 1962. Australian Broadcasting Commission. *The Canberra Times*, 1 January, p. 9.

Australian Jazz Museum, 2015. *The Cool School of the 1950s – The Beginning of Modern Jazz in Australia – (2 CD Set) AJM 034 – CSO 690* [Online] Available at: https://www.ajm.org.au/?product=034-the-cool-school-of-the-1950s-the-beginning-of-modern-jazz-in-australia-2-cd-set-ajm-034-cso-690 [Accessed 21 July 2025].

Australian Jazz Museum, n.d. *Australian Jazz Museum* [Online] Available at: http://ajm.melbourne.axiell.com/?page=search#view=list&id=1a38&terms=%5B%22and%22%2C%5B%5B%22and%22%2C%5B%5D%5D%2C%5B%22keywords%22%2C%221960%20jazz%20festival%22%5D%2C%5B%22and%22%2C%5B%5B%22record-purpose%22%2C%22imu%20navigation%22%2C%22%3C%3E%22%5D%5D%5D [Accessed 20 July 2025].

Baker, A., 1960a. Listen Here. *Teenagers' Weekly*, 9 November, p. 11.

Baker, A., 1960b. Jazz Goes to College. *Teenager's Weekly*, 21 September, p. 6.

BBC, 1964. *Jazz 625: Marian McPartland* [Online] Available at: https://genome.ch.bbc.co.uk/27d6309de6cb483aac69f759a39b2ef5 [Accessed 22 July 2025].

BBC, 1965a. *Jazz Club* [Online] Available at: https://genome.ch.bbc.co.uk/266d36b613f04986adfbe40c9a431bf9 [Accessed 22 July 2025].

BBC, 1965b. *Jazz Club* [Online] Available at: https://genome.ch.bbc.co.uk/04c947a39825419abcde08118e0916e8 [Accessed 22 July 2025].

BBC, 1967. *The Jazz Scene* [Online] Available at: https://genome.ch.bbc.co.uk/9a69acebcad545a89cab5884af871136 [Accessed 22 July 2025].

Be! Records, 2016a. *The Three Out – Move* [Online] Available at: https://web.archive.org/web/20160627025604/http://www.negamusi.com:80/product/the-three-out-move [Accessed 21 July 2015].

Be! Records, 2016b. *The Three Out – Sittin' in with the Three Out* [Online] Available at: https://web.archive.org/web/20160629133813/http://www.negamusi.com:80/product/the-three-out-sittin-in-with-the-three-out/ [Accessed 21 July 2025].

Beck, P., 1982. *De Pia Beck story*. Amsterdam: Tiebosch Uitgeversmaatschappij bv.

Beek, P., n.d. *Johnny & Jones* [Online] Available at: https://holocaustmusic.ort.org/places/camps/western-europe/westerbork/johnny-jones/ [Accessed 18 July 2025].

Bell, G., 1952. Contemporary European Jazz. *ABC Weekly*, 29 November, p. 29.

Bell, G., 1988. *Graeme Bell, Australian Jazzman: His Autobiography*. Frenchs Forest, New South Wales: Child & Associates.

Berg, C., 1978. Mike Nock. *Down Beat*, 23 March, p. 18.

Beyond El Rocco, 1990. [Film] Directed by Kevin Lucas. Australia: Ronin Films.

Bhatt, J., 2024. *Jazz Pianist Mike Nock to Be Inducted into NZ Music Hall of Fame* [Online] Available at: https://www.rnz. co.nz/news/national/525935/jazz-pianist-mike-nock-to-be-inducted-into-nz-music-hall-of-fame [Accessed 19 July 2025].

Bird's Basement, 2016. *Mike Nock Trio* [Online] Available at: https:// web.archive.org/web/20160401000344/http://birdsbasement. com/show/26/mike-nock-trio- [Accessed 21 July 2025].

Bisset, A., 1987. *Black Roots, White Flowers: A History of Jazz in Australia*. 2nd ed. Sydney: ABC Enterprises.

Blum, K., 2018. *Horst Liepolt, the Man Who Helped Build a Brand for Australian Jazz* [Online] Available at: https://australianjazz. net/2018/12/horst-liepolt-man-helped-build-brand-australian-jazz/ [Accessed 11 August 2025].

Blum, K., 2019. 'Jazz Forever' Vale Horst Liepolt – Artist and Jazz Producer, Australia and USA. *AJazz*, February (81), pp. 12–13.

Bollinger, N., 2020. *Arthur Pearce aka Cotton-Eyed Joe, Turntable* [Online] Available at: https://www.audioculture.co.nz/profile/ arthur-pearce [Accessed 19 July 2025].

Boothroyd, D., 1978. Chris Karan's Expresso Bongos. *Melody Maker*, 53(29), p. 40.

Bourke, C., 2013. *Blue Smoke: The Lost Dawn of New Zealand Popular Music, 1918–1964*. Auckland: Auckland University Press.

Brennan, G., 1988. El Rocco Knockout. *The Sydney Morning Herald*, 3 August, p. 18.

Brennan, G., 1994. Nock of Narawokia. *The Sydney Morning Herald The Guide*, 24 October, p. 17s.

Brian Brown Quintet, T., 1977. *Brian Brown Quintet 1958* [Sound Recording] (44 Records).

Brown, R., 1957. New Jazz Club for Sydney. *Music Maker*, January, p. 25.

Caddy, B., 2022. *Interview by Email* [Interview] (30 November 2022).

Caddy, B., 2023. *Interview in Cambridge* [Interview] (28 March 2023).

Cale, B., 2022. *Interview by Telephone* [Interview] (1 September 2022).

Canberra Times, T., 2006. *A Jazz Legend Returns* [Online] Available at: https://www.proquest.com/newspapers/jazz-legend-returns-arts-entertainment/docview/1018846961/se-2 [Accessed 19 July 2025].

Caplice, P., 2022. *Interview by Phone* [Interview] (27 August 2022).

Carlyon, J., 2013. *Changing Times: New Zealand since 1945*. Auckland: Auckland University Press.

Civic Theatre, 1961. Advertisement: Jazz Concert. *The Press*, 14 April, p. 1.

Clare, J. & Brennan, G., 1995. *Bodgie Dada & the Cult of Cool: Australian Jazz since 1945*. Sydney: University of New South Wales.

Clayton, P., 1966. Jazz. *The Sunday Telegraph*, 28 August, p. 9.

Clifton, T., 1966. Jazz. *Daily Mail*, 18 March, p. 18.

Club 43, 1961. Advertisement: Dankworth All Stars. *Manchester Evening News*, 22 September, p. 2.

Conte, N., 2004. *Nicola Conte* [Online] Available at: https://nowtoronto.com/music/nicola-conte-2004-04-01/ [Accessed 26 July 2025].

Czyz, K., 1979. Mike Nock. *Jazz Forum*, 59(3), pp. 50–1.

D.W.R., 1961. Three Out Trio – Enjoyable Jazz Concert. *The Press*, April, p. 20.

Davis, C. T. & Spillett, S., 2015. *100% Proof: The Complete Tubby Hayes Discography*. Almere, Netherlands: Names & Numbers.

De Looper, M., 2014. *Coronet & CBS EP's & LP'S 1956–1986* [Online] Available at: https://www.australianrecordlabels.com/wp-content/uploads/2014/10/CORONET-CBS-EPS-LPS-1956-1986.pdf [Accessed 19 August 2025].

De Looper, M., 2024. *Australian Concert Tours 1950–1979* [Online] Available at: https://australianrecordlabels.com/wp-content/uploads/2024/11/Australian-tours-1950-1979.pdf [Accessed 20 July 2025].

De Looper, M., 2025a. *E.M.I. (Australia) Ltd. Columbia* [Online] Available at: https://australianrecordlabels.com/wp-content/uploads/2025/04/Columbia.pdf [Accessed 20 July 2025].

De Looper, M., 2025b. *E.M.M. (Australia) Ltd. Budget Labels, Compilations and Consolidated L.P. Series* [Online] Available at: https://australianrecordlabels.com/wp-content/uploads/2025/04/Budget-Compilation-Consolidated-LPs.pdf [Accessed 21 July 2025].

De Telegraaf, 1953. Familieberichten. *De Telegraaf*, 9 October, p. 8.

De Zaanlander van Dinsdag, 1948. Jazz-Parade Een Succes. *De Zaanlander van Dinsdag*, 30 November, p. 3.

Dean, R., Pressing, J. & Whiteoak, J., 2025. *Rohde, Bryce (Benno)* [Online] Available at: https://doi.org/10.1093/gmo/9781561592630.article.J384400 [Accessed 12 August 2025].

DeVeaux, S., 1997. *The Birth of Bebop: A Social and Musical History*. California: University of California.

Devlin, J., 1958. *How Would 'Ya Be* [Sound Recording] (Prestige Records).

Discogs, 2024. *Recent Sales History The 3 Out – Move (Columbia, Columbia) LP, Album, Mono* [Online] Available at: https://www.discogs.com/sell/history/8658177 [Accessed 26 July 2025].

Discogs, 2025a. *Columbia Graphophone (Aust.) Ltd.* [Online] Available at: https://www.discogs.com/label/577867-Columbia-Graphophone-Aust-Ltd?redirected=true&genre=Jazz [Accessed 19 July 2025].

Discogs, 2025b. *Jazz in Australia* [Online] Available at: https://www.discogs.com/label/1619629-Jazz-In-Australia [Accessed 20 July 2025].

Discogs, 2025c. *Don Burrows* [Online] Available at: https://www.discogs.com/artist/147910-Don-Burrows?superFilter=Credits [Accessed 22 July 2025].

Discogs, 2025d. *Chris Karan* [Online] Available at: https://www.discogs.com/artist/317436-Chris-Karan?superFilter=Credits [Accessed 27 July 2025].

Disk Union, n.d. *The Australian All Stars* [Online] Available at: https://diskunion.net/jazz/ct/list/0/72359301 [Accessed 21 July 2025].

Down Beat, 1961. Down Beat Hall of Fame Scholarships-1961. *Down Beat*, 28(13), p. 15.

Downbeat, 1957a. Australian Jazzmen Rock U.S. *The Sun-Herald*, 18 August, p. 60.

Downbeat, 1957b. Robeson Is Heard Again. *The Sunday Herald*, 22 September, p. 76.

Downbeat, 1958. Cool Brew of Local Jazz. *The Sun-Herald*, 16 March, p. 84.

Downbeat, 1959. Witchcraft and Cups of Tea Make an LP. *The Sun-Herald*, 16 August, p. 102.

Downbeat, 1960a. A Weird Mob of Play LPs. *The Sun-Herald*, 15 May, p. 110.

Downbeat, 1960b. Jazz Jumps the Pacific. *The Sun-Herald*, 13 November, p. 93.

Downbeat, 1960c. Big Smoke and Country Jazz. *The Sun-Herald*, 12 June, p. 73.

Downbeat, 1960d. The Girl Too Good to Sell …. *The Sun-Herald*, July(24), p. 91.

Downbeat, 1960e. Aussie Jazz – Several Degrees Warm …. *The Sun-Herald*, 16 October, p. 97.

Downbeat, 1961a. Brubeck Meets a Shouter. *The Sun-Herald*, 5 March, p. 77.

Downbeat, 1961b. An Ear Bashing from a Dinkum Aussie. *The Sun-Herald*, 3 December, p. 95.

Dusty Groove, Inc., n.d.a. *Three Out (Mike Nock)* [Online] Available at: https://www.dustygroove.com/item/775772/Three-Out-Mike-Nock-:Move [Accessed 21 July 2025].

Dusty Groove, Inc., n.d.b. *Three Out (Mike Nock)* [Online] Available at: https://www.dustygroove.com/item/775771/Three-Out-Mike-Nock-:Sittin-In [Accessed 21 July 2025].

Dutch Australian Weekly, 1956. Freddy Loggen thans voor ABC televisie. *Dutch Australian Weekly*, 2 November, p. 3.

Dyer, M., 1960. International Jazz Festival. *Jazz Notes* (106), p. 4.

Egan, M., 2008. *Interview with Votary Records' James Pianta* [Online] Available at: http://aussiefunk.blogspot.com/2008/02/

interview-with-votary-records-james.html [Accessed 21 July 2025].

El Rocco, 1960. Advertisement – Jazz Jazz Jazz Jazz. *The Sydney Morning Herald*, 21 May, p. 24.

Elwood, P., 1968. 'The 4th Way' Jazzmen. *The San Francisco Examiner*, 10 September, p. 27.

European Stars and Stripes, 1954. An Evening with Anne Nicolas. *European Stars and Stripes Feature Section*, 11 July, p. XI.

Farbey, R., 2005. *Tubby Hayes: Tubby Hayes: Mexican Green* [Online] Available at: https://www.allaboutjazz.com/tubby-hayes-mexican-green-by-roger-farbey [Accessed 8 September 2025].

Fats, 1949. *The 45 Jam Club News*, 15 March, p. 1.

Feldman, R., 1961. Dianas Got 'Butterflies'. *The Australian Women's Weekly*, 3 August, p. 7.

Fisher, D. & Somerville, J., 1961a. Around Town. *Music Maker*, August, p. 4.

Fisher, D. & Somerville, J., 1961b. Around Town. *Music Maker*, December, p. 5.

Ford, J., Higgins, G., Lansley, B. & Walters, R., 1960. Untitled. *The Odd Note*, 2(4), pp. 12–16.

Forge, K., 2025. *London Is Home to One of the Most Famous Jazz Clubs in the World – And It Has Just Been Named the UK's Most Popular Independent Music Venue* [Online] Available at: https://secretldn.com/ronnie-scotts-best-independent-music-venue-uk/ [Accessed 13 August 2025].

Foster, M., 1971. The Name Is Moore. *The Canberra Times*, 20 January, p. 27.

Gammond, P., 1976. *Scott Joplin and the Ragtime Era*. Revised ed. New York: St. Martin's Press.

Gillespie, B., 2025. *Interview by Phone* [Interview] (26 July 2025).

Gitler, I., 1985. *Swing to Bop: An Oral History of the Transition in Jazz in the 1940s*. New York: Oxford University Press.

Giuffre, L., 2016. The Lost History of Jazz on Early Australian Popular Music Television. In: B. Johnson, ed. *Antipodean Riffs: Essays on Australasian jazz*. Sheffield, South Yorkshire: Equinox Publishing, pp. 117–34.

Global Recording Artists, n.d. *Accent Records Discography* [Online] Available at: http://gragroup.com/accent/discography1950s45rpm.html [Accessed 20 July 2025].

Godbolt, J., 1984. *A History of Jazz in Britain, 1919–1950*. London: Quartet Books.

Gottschalk, M., 2025. *Interview by Phone* [Interview] (18 January 2025).

Green, G., 1978. Keyboard Workshops. *The Sun-Herald*, 2 April, p. 80.

Grigg, S., n.d. *Zodiac 45s* [Online] Available at: https://www.simongrigg.info/zodiac.htm [Accessed 19 July 2025].

Hall, E., 1959. Brisbane Bandwagon – Frank Thornton Group. *Music Maker*, April, p. 34.

Harris, R., 1957. *Jazz*. 5th ed. Middlesex: Penguin Books.

Hart, G., 1959. Sinatra, Freberg – 'Sheer Delight'. *Music Maker*, May, p. 7.

Hart, G., 1960. Australian All-Stars. *Australian Music Maker and Dance Band News*, June, p. 29.

Hawkins, C. & Ramblers, T., 1968. *The Hawk in Holland* [Sound Recording] (Ace of Clubs).

Heathcote, R., 2008. *Jazz Trumpeter Urged Youth to Keep It Real* [Online] Available at: https://www.smh.com.au/national/jazz-trumpeter-urged-youth-to-keep-it-real-20080820-gdsrhl.html [Accessed 21 July 2025].

Heffernan, A., 2003. *Big Shows: The Lee Gordon Years*. Clear Island Waters, Queensland: Alan Heffernan.

Hennessey, M., 1965. Jazz Fest Ripples with Rhythm. *Billboard*, 77(47), p. 24.

Hentoff, N., 1953. Jazz Reviews. *Down Beat*, 20(26), p. 14.

Hentoff, N., 1955. Jazz from Down Under. *Down Beat*, 22(1), p. 14.

Heppie, P., 1983. Sheraton Skyline. *The Stage and Television Today*, 21 April, p. 5.

Hessey, R., 1987. El-Rocco Is Born Again – and All That Jazz. *Eastern Herald*, 29 October, p. 11.

Hi Fi Stereophonie, 1971. He Mike Nock Underground / Between or Beyond. *Hi Fi Stereophonie*, October, p. 923.

hrd, 1953. Freddy Loggen and His Quintet. *Philharmonic*, 4(8), p. 14.

Hughes, D., 1977. *Daddy's Practising Again: An Australian Jazzman Looks Back and Around*. Richmond, Victoria: Marlin Books.

Hughes, D., 1980. Hard Music by a Kiwi Star. *The Sydney Mirror*, 2 July.

Isackson, L., 1960. *Isackson, Leon: HM03: Jazz at the Stadium 1960: Home Movie* [Online] Available at: https://www.collection.nfsa. gov.au/title/801393 [Accessed 20 July 2025].

Jackson, A., 1978. Moore, Maestro of the Madcap. *The Age Weekender*, 14 April, p. 5.

Jackson, A., 1979. Mike Wants to Jazz Up Our Lives. *The Age*, 17 February, p. 19.

Jackson, A., 1984. Many Happy Harper Returns. *The Age Weekender*, 6 April, p. 2.

Jazz News, 1961. News Round-Up. *Jazz News*, 5(27), p. 4.

Jazz News, 1962. Tubby's New Group for Scott Club Debut. *Jazz News*, 6(5), p. 3.

Jewell, D., 1964. Trombone Trumps. *The Sunday Times*, 30 August, p. 26.

Johnson, B., 1983a. *The El Rocco: An Era in Sydney Jazz* [Online] Available at: https://static1.squarespace.com/static/58bf64e6c534a5e3ac61401d/t/59da3b3a197aea8dd94e3600/1507474247327/JohnsonBruceTHEELROCCO.pdf [Accessed 20 July 2025].

Johnson, B., 1983b. *The Sydney Jazz Club: 30 Years On* [Online] Available at: https://static1.squarespace.com/static/58bf64e6c534a5e3ac61401d/t/598d5407d7bdceac688db0c2/1502434317531/JohnsonBruceSYDNEYJAZZCLUB.pdf [Accessed 20 July 2025].

Johnson, B., 1987. *The Oxford Companion to Jazz*. Melbourne: Oxford University Press.

Jones, C., 2024. *Interview by Phone* [Interview] (25 June 2024).

K.M., 1962. Brubeck Consolidates Jazz Reputation. *The Sydney Morning Herald*, 31 March, p. 17.

Karan, C., 2022a. *Interview by Phone* [Interview] (18 March 2022a).

Karan, C., 2022b. *Interview by Phone about Jazz Clubs* [Interview] (22 September 2022b).

Karan, C., 2025. *Interview by Phone* [Interview] (23 May 2025).

Kee, J., 2016. *Three Out Redux Australian Jazz History Reprised* [Online] Available at: http://jazz.org.au/three-out-redux-australian-jazz-history-reprised/ [Accessed 30 August 2024].

Kennedy, I. & Courtenay, B., 1995. *The Power of One to One*. Double Bay, New South Wales: Margaret Gee Publishing.

Kennedy, J., 2015. Research Review. *VJazz* (65), pp. 11–12.

Kenny, J., 2025. *The Tubby Hayes Quintet – Antibes '62* [Online] Available at: https://jazzviews.net/the-tubby-hayes-quintet-antibes-62/ [Accessed 9 August 2025].

Kinsella, R., 2022. *The Bebop Scene in London's Soho, 1945–1950 Post-war Britain's First Youth Subculture*. Cham, Switzerland: Palgrave Macmillan.

Kleinhout, H., 2006. *Jazz als probleem. Receptie en acceptatie van de jazz in de wederopbouwperiode van Nederland 1945–1952* [Online] Available at: https://dspace.library.uu.nl/handle/1874/12366 [Accessed 19 July 2025].

L.D.H., 1960. Brubeck Quartet Concert. *The Sydney Morning Herald*, 19 March, p. 6.

Langlands, P., 2022. *Interview by Email* [Interview] (18 April 2022).

Lawson, L., 1961. The Sydney Spotlight. *Music Maker*, February, 6(9), p. 7.

Lawson, L. & Somerville, J., 1960. Around Town. *Music Maker*, December, pp. 4–5.

Lawson, L. & Somerville, J., 1961a. Around Town. *Music Maker*, February, 6(9), p. 4.

Lawson, L. & Somerville, J., 1961b. Around Town. *Music Maker*, March, p. 5.

Lawson, L. & Somerville, J., 1961c. Around Town. *Music Maker*, May, p. 5.

Lawson, L. & Somerville, J., 1961d. Around Town. *Music Maker*, June, p. 7.

Lee, A., 1961. Melbourne Roundup. *Music Maker*, April, p. 19.

Lee Gordon, 1960a. *1st Annual Australian International Jazz Festival*. Sydney: Publicity Press Pty.

Lee Gordon, 1960b. Advertisement: Lee Gordon Presents 1st Annual Australian International Jazz Festival. *The Sydney Morning Herald*, 17 September, p. 23.

Lee Gordon, 1960c. Advertisement: Lee Gordon Presents: First Australian International Jazz Festival. *The Sydney Morning Herald*, 8 October, p. 24.

Lee Gordon, 1960d. Advertisement: The Pigalle Theatre Restaurant. *The Sun-Herald*, 30 October, p. 45.

Leerink, J. A., 1950. PIA BECK kan geen noot lezen: Eerste Nederlandse Artiste voor de Engelse Televisie. *De Telegraaf*, 5 September, p. 5.

Lewis, A. & Lewis, L., 1992. Mike Nock Interview. *Cadence*, 18(7), pp. 11–18.

Logan, F., 1965. *Freddy Logan's Afro Cuban Big Band – In Concert BBC Jazz Club* [Sound Recording] (BBC Jazz Club).

Loggen, F., 1951. Commentaar Op Het Artikel Van M.A. De Ruyter Over Bop En New Orleans Jazz. *The 45 Club News*, 3(1), pp. 7–8.

Lord, T., 1992. *The Jazz Discography Volume 2*. West Vancouver: Lord Music Reference.

Lord, T., 1993. *The Jazz Discography: Volume 7*. West Vancouver: Lord Music Reference Inc.

Lord, T., 1994a. *The Jazz Discography Volume 8*. West Vancouver: Lord Music Reference Inc.

Lord, T., 1994b. *The Jazz Discography Volume 10*. West Vancouver: Lord Music Reference Inc.

Lord, T., 2001. *The Jazz Discography Volume 25*. West Vancouver: Lord Music Reference Inc.

Male, A., 2021. *'Rawness, Freedom, Experimentation': The Brit Jazz Boom of the 60s and 70s* [Online] Available at: https://www.theguardian.com/music/2021/aug/18/rawness-freedom-experimentation-british-jazz-john-surman-tony-higgins [Accessed 13 August 2025].

Mandel, H., 2019. *Jazz & Blues Encyclopedia: New & Expanded Edition.* 2nd ed. London: Flame Tree Publishing.

McBeath, J., 2015. *Memorable Moments Abound as Legendary Saxophonist Errol Buddle Celebrated the Career of Bruce Hancock* [Online] Available at: https://www.adelaidenow.com.au/entertainment/arts/memorable-moments-abound-as-legendary-saxophonist-errol-buddle-celebrated-the-career-of-bruce-hancock/news-story/49c3211f21b65f3b8cc6c7535285715e [Accessed 21 July 2025].

McFadzean, D. M. & Churchward, M., 2009. *Post World War II Migrant Ship History: Patris, 1959–1975* [Online] Available at: https://collections.museumsvictoria.com.au/articles/15589 [Accessed 21 July 2025].

Mckay, G., 2012. *Interview with Drummer Colin Bailey, Who Worked with Winifred Atwell in the 1950s* [Online] Available at: https://salford-repository.worktribe.com/output/1437673/interview-with-drummer-colin-bailey-who-worked-with-winifred-atwell-in-the-1950s [Accessed 18 August 2025].

Meehan, N., 2010. *Serious Fun: The Life and Music of Mike Nock.* Wellington: Te Herenga Waka University Press.

Meyer, J., 2024. *Sounds Visual Radio Episode 182: Mike Nock* [Online] Available at: https://www.soundsvisualradio.com/podcast/episode-182-mike-nock/ [Accessed 26 July 2025].

Miliano, M., 2012. On the Occasion of ASRA's Silver Jubilee. *The Australasian Sound Archive* (37), pp. 17–56.

Mitchell, J., 1988. *Australian Jazz on Record, 1925–80*. Canberra: AGPS Press.

Moore, D., 1962. *Plays the Theme from Beyond the Fringe & All That Jazz* [Sound Recording] (Atlantic).

Morcombe, J., 2021. *Confused about Freshwater vs Harbord? Then Add Dee Why* [Online] Available at: https://www. dailytelegraph.com.au/newslocal/manly-daily/confused-about-freshwater-vs-harbord-then-add-dee-why/news-story/208f23eef1dd03a655a57275bbc9449c [Accessed 27 July 2025].

Morgan, A., 1959. Pat Caplice Quartet. *The Gramophone Supplement*, January, p. 381.

Mr Kokomo, n.d. *The Amazing Brass Section* [Online] Available at: http://www.mrkokomo.bizhosting.com/brass.htm [Accessed 21 July 2025].

Music for Your Ears, 2023. *1st Annual Australian International Jazz Festival (1960)* [Online] Available at: https:// youtube.com/playlist?list=PLk3g8XK3O-qSOglxFTqXK-G0jUQwB7k6V&si=IMU-ECad7HARMuQN [Accessed 20 July 2025].

Music Maker, 1956. Overseas Stylists Settle Here. *Music Maker*, November, p. 27.

Music Maker, 1957a. New Site for Club 11. *Music Maker*, March, p. 24.

Music Maker, 1957b. Musicians Formed This Jazz Club – And Its Thriving!. *Music Maker*, June, p. 26.

Music Maker, 1957c. New Jazz Club Is Here to Stay. *Music Maker*, February, p. 25.

Music Maker, 1957d. 1957 Australian Musicians' Poll Vote Now for Your Favourites!. *Music Maker*, April, p. 5.

Music Maker, 1957e. 'M.M.' Readers Name Winners in 1957 Australian Musicians' Poll. *Music Maker*, July, p. 1.

Music Maker, 1957f. 'M.M.' Musicians' Poll Winners Make Disc for Parlophone Series. *Music Maker*, August, p. 3.

Music Maker, 1957g. Men at Work. …. *Music Maker*, September, pp. 12–13, 34.

Music Maker, 1958a. 'Jazz for Pleasure' from A.B.C. *Music Maker*, June, p. 2.

Music Maker, 1958b. ABC Jazz Show Scores a Hit. *Music Maker*, July, p. 3.

Music Maker, 1958c. Sydney Spotlight. *Music Maker*, July, p. 35.

Music Maker, 1958d. 'Jazz College' on Television. *Music Maker*, May, p. 2.

Music Maker, 1958e. Don Burrows Group Makes Disc. *Music Maker*, May, p. 3.

Music Maker, 1960a. New LP by Sydney Jazz Group. *Music Maker*, June, p. 3.

Music Maker, 1960b. Record Reviews – Jazz. *Music Maker*, September, p. 25.

Music Maker, 1960c. Australian Group Plans a Local 'Jazz Goes to College' Tour. *Music Maker*, June, p. 5.

Music Maker, 1960d. 'Three-Out' Record For E.M.I. *Music Maker*, November, p. 4.

Music Maker, 1960e. 3-Out at Primitif. *Music Maker*, October, p. 4.

Music Maker, 1960f. Sydney Jazz Scene. *Music Maker*, December, 6(9), p. 31.

Music Maker, 1961. Sydney Jazz Scene. *Music Maker*, April, p. 37.

Myers, E., 1981. Jazz Improvisor Returns for Renewal. *The Sydney Morning Herald*, 12 May, p. 8.

Myers, E., 2018. *Adelaide's Errol Buddle Scaled Heights of American Jazz* [Online] Available at: https://www.theaustralian.com.au/arts/music/adelaides-erol-buddle-scaled-heights-of-american-jazz/news-story/58539722192318c8ecafe6d5a03fd589 [Accessed 21 July 2025].

Myers, E., n.d. *Ron Falson: Crash Hot Jazz Players* [Online] Available at: https://static1.squarespace.com/static/58bf64e6c534a5e3ac61401d/t/5e43fc87812434757a57ff85/1581514034386/MyersEricCrashHotJazzPlayersRonFalson.pdf [Accessed 21 July 2025].

Myers, M., 1974. Vacation Memories …. *Palm Desert Post*, 10 October, pp. B–1.

Nationaal Archief, n.d. *Jan Loggen* [Online] Available at: https://www.nationaalarchief.nl/onderzoeken/index/nt00475/AE178415 [Accessed 21 July 2025].

National Film and Sound Archive of Australia, 1960. *Move: [Master Tapes]* [Online] Available at: https://www.collection.nfsa.gov.au/title/541585 [Accessed 20 July 2025].

National Film and Sound Archive of Australia, 1998. *The First Wave: Australian Rock and Pop Recordings (1955–1963)* [Online] Available at: https://www.nfsa.gov.au/sites/default/files/11-2016/nfsa_the_first_wave_aust_1955_1963_amended.pdf [Accessed 20 July 2025].

National Library of Australia, n.d. *Weston, Billy* [Online] Available at: https://trove.nla.gov.au/people/1462015 [Accessed 20 July 2025].

National Library Wellington, 1960. *Music Programmes 1960* [Online] Available at: https://natlib.govt.nz/records/22576790 [Accessed 20 July 2025].

Nederlands Jazz Archief, n.d.a. *1939–1945 Oorlog, Bezetting en Bevrijding* [Online] Available at: https://www.jazzhelden.nl/

action/front/history;jsessionid=1687C89E513D2D455021913F
B524F0A4?start=1939 [Accessed 18 July 2025].

Nederlands Jazz Archief, n.d.b. *1920–1939 Nederland omarmt jazz*
[Online] Available at: https://www.jazzhelden.nl/action/front/
history?start=1920 [Accessed 18 July 2025].

Netherlands Institute for War Documentation, 2024. *Camps
in the Netherlands* [Online] Available at: https://www.
kamparchieven.nl/en/camps-in-the-netherlands [Accessed 21
July 2025].

Nettelbeck, T., 2017. *Frank Smith at the Embers, Melbourne 1960–61*
[Online] Available at: https://static1.squarespace.com/
static/58bf64e6c534a5e3ac61401d/t/5a3aea65085229aa04ea
0b02/1513810541995/NettelbeckTedFrankSmithAtTheEmbers.
pdf [Accessed 2 August 2025].

Nettelbeck, T., 2020. *Some Memories of Bassist Freddy Logan*
[Online] Available at: https://static1.squarespace.com/
static/58bf64e6c534a5e3ac61401d/t/5f31432fdf524e64bc3d
96cf/1597063995765/NettelbeckTedFreddieLoganMemoir.pdf
[Accessed 19 July 2025].

Nettelbeck, T., 2022. *Interview by Phone* [Interview] (13 December
2022).

Newcastle Morning Herald and Miners' Advocate, 1954. Winifred
Atwell for Australia. *Newcastle Morning Herald and Miners'
Advocate*, 18 March, p. 9.

Nicholas, P., 1954. Winifred Atwell Girl with the Golden Touch. *The
World's News*, 25 December, pp. 7–8.

Nock, M., 2004. *Mike Nock Trio* [Online] Available at: https://
webarchive.nla.gov.au/awa/20050626054747/http://www.
jazz-planet.com/artman/publish/article_4.shtml [Accessed 21
July 2025].

Nock, M., 2015. *Facebook* [Online] Available at: https://www.
   facebook.com/photo/?fbid=983166821755110&set
   =a.615008678570928 [Accessed 21 July 2025].

Nock, M., 2016a. *Facebook* [Online] Available at: https://www.
   facebook.com/mikenockmusic/posts/pfbid0okQwrr4obkDp
   B8wjRUENUE4vmd76FNaZpuDDSvseWhKXhndu9wvENvBGdr
   8oyPLDl [Accessed 21 July 2025].

Nock, M., 2016b. *Facebook* [Online] Available at: https://www.
   facebook.com/photo/?fbid=1035514223187036&set
   =a.615008678570928 [Accessed 21 July 2025].

Nock, M., 2019. *2019–12–03 Mike Nock Trio* [Sound Recording].

Nock, M., 2022. *Interview by Phone* [Interview] (17 March 2022).

Nock, M., 2024. *Interview In-Person in Sydney* [Interview] (17 July 2024).

Nock, M. & Karan, C., 2025. *Interviews by Email* [Interview] (17 July
   2025).

Nuttall, L., 2025. *Tony Worsley – Velvet Waters (1965)* [Online]
   Available at: https://poparchives.com.au/tony-worsley/velvet-
   waters/ [Accessed 27 July 2025].

NZ Listener, 1962. Hot and Swinging. *NZ Listener*, 16 March.

O'Connell, D., 2021. *Harlem Nights: The Secret History of Australia's
   Jazz Age*. eBook ed. Melbourne: Melbourne University Press.

O'Regan, J. & Byron, T., 2024. The Development of the Australian
   Pop Charts and the Changing Meaning of the 'Number
   One' Single. In: C. Bracknell & A. Harris, eds. *The Cambridge
   Companion to Music in Australia*. Cambridge: Cambridge
   University Press, pp. 148–61.

Ölscher, T., 2024. *Interview by Email* [Interview] (9 September 2024).

Openneer, H., 1996. Overleden Jan Blok. *Jazz Bulletin*, March (19),
   p. 17.

Oxley, G. L., 2003. *A Ceremony for Frederick Christian Logan in Celebration of His Life and in Farewell at His Death*. s.l.: The British Humanist Association.

Page, G., 1997. *Bernie McGann: A Life in Jazz*. Armidale, New South Wales: Kardoorair Press.

Page, G., 2025. *Interview by Email* [Interview] (4–5 January 2025).

Paskin, B., 2000. *Dudley Moore: The Melancholy Clown*. 2nd ed. California: New Millennium Press.

Pitt, K., 1950. Ken Pitt Reports from London. *Philharmonic*, November, p. 264.

Pollard, A. C., 1950. Index to Volume XXVII June 1949 to May 1950. *The Gramophone*, XXVII, pp. 24, 28.

Powerhouse, 1959. *'Jimmie Rodgers' Concert Program* [Online] Available at: https://collection.powerhouse.com.au/object/164454 [Accessed 19 July 2025].

Pozza, E., 2019. *Nothing to Prove* [Online] Available at: https://canberrajazz.blogspot.com/2019/12/nothing-to-prove.html?m=0 [Accessed 21 July 2025].

Presley, F., 2016. *Interviews with* [Online] Available at: http://www.jazzandbeyond.com.au/sound/MikeNock3.mp3 [Accessed 27 December 2024].

Promethean Editions, 2024. *Mike Nock* [Online] Available at: https://www.prometheaneditions.com/php/ComposerSummary.php?CompID=28 [Accessed 25 July 2025].

Rawlins, A., 1961. Three Out Trio. *The Bulletin*, 29 March, p. 47.

Rechniewski, P., 1983. *The Crisis in Modern Jazz in Australia* [Online] Available at: https://static1.squarespace.com/static/58bf64e6c534a5e3ac61401d/t/5af7e0532b6a287aca2ea5e2/1526194273606/RechniewskiPCrisisInModernJazz.pdf [Accessed 21 July 2025].

Reid, G., 2024. *Mike Nock: The Jazz Career That Led to NZ Music Hall of Fame* [Online] Available at: https://www.nzherald. co.nz/the-listener/entertainment/pioneering-jazz-artist-mike-nock-inducted-into-the-nz-music-hall-of-fame/ YOCVOLVZKZEQRLTKAYSI7UICUA/ [Accessed 19 July 2025].

RHMS Patris, 1961a. Advertisement: RHMS Patris. *The Age*, 8 May, p. 7.

RHMS Patris, 1961b. RHMS Patris. *The Sydney Morning Herald*, 12 May, p. 20.

Rhythme, 1953a. Spotlight. *Rhythme* (43), p. 12.

Rhythme, 1953b. Levende Muziek. *Rhythme*, 4(45), p. 6.

Rippin, J. W., 1948. Recorded Jazz in Australia. *The Jazzfinder*, 1(7), p. 20.

Rippin, J. W., 1949. Emergence of the Australian Style. In: *The Jazz Finder '49*. New Orleans: Playback, pp. 25–30.

Roberts, M., 2014. *The Rex Hotel Empire* [Online] Available at: https://timegents.com/2014/11/22/the-rex-hotels/ [Accessed 11 August 2025].

Robson, A., 2021. *Austral Jazz: The Localization of a Global Music Form in Sydney*. New York: Routledge.

Rolfe, P., 1954. She Can Write Her Own Ticket for Foreign Travel. *The Australian Women's Weekly*, 1 December, p. 41.

Rozek, M., 1977. Profile Mike Nock. *Down Beat*, 44(7), pp. 35–6.

Ryan, G., 2024. *Australian Singles Charts 1940 to 2020*, s.l.: Gavin Ryan.

S.S., 1952a. Big LP Drive Beginning. *The Sunday Herald*, 13 July, p. 12.

S.S., 1952b. Playing a Record Is Harder Now. *The Sunday Herald*, 15 June, p. 10.

S.S., 1952c. Local LP Issues Begin. *The Sunday Herald*, 30 November, p. 12.

S.S., 1954. Many More Good Records This Year. *The Sunday Herald*, 10 January, p. 74.

Sam, B. J. M., 1952. Smash!. *Philharmonic*, 3(7), p. 134.

Scott-Maxwell, A. & Whiteoak, J. eds., 2003. *Currency Companion to Music and Dance in Australia*. Strawberry Hills, New South Wales: Currency House Inc.

SecondHandSongs, 2025a. *Autumn in New York* [Online] Available at: https://secondhandsongs.com/work/76498/versions [Accessed 15 November 2025].

SecondHandSongs, 2025b. *Softly, as in a Morning Sunrise* [Online] Available at: https://secondhandsongs.com/work/9704/all [Accessed 15 November 2025].

SecondHandSongs, 2025c. *Subtle Slough*. [Online] Available at: https://secondhandsongs.com/work/138998/versions [Accessed 7 December 2025].

Shand, J., 2009. *Jazz: The Australian Accent*. Sydney: UNSW Press.

Shand, J., 2016. The Original Hipsters. *The Sydney Morning Herald*, 28 May, p. 20.

Shand, J., 2018. *Errol Buddle Story: World's First Jazz Bassoonist Was a Hit in the US* [Online] Available at: https://www.smh.com.au/entertainment/music/errol-buddle-story-worlds-first-jazz-bassoonist-was-a-hit-in-the-us-20180301-h0wtjj.html [Accessed 21 July 2025].

Shand, J., 2020. *Musician Did More than Anyone to Popularise Jazz in Australia* [Online] Available at: https://www.smh.com.au/national/musician-did-more-than-anyone-to-popularise-jazz-in-australia-20200325-p54dnq.html [Accessed 22 August 2025].

Shand, J., 2023. *This Jazz Legend's First Solo Album in 30 Years Is Worth the Wait* [Online] Available at: https://www.smh.com.au/culture/music/best-new-music-to-listen-to-in-september-20230828-p5e02p.html [Accessed 9 August 2025].

Sharpe, J., 2008. *I Wanted to Be a Jazz Musician*. Torrens, A.C.T.: John Sharpe.

Sloggett, J., 2024. *Interview by Phone* [Interview] (2 July 2024).

Smith's Alternative, 2019. *Geoff's Jazz at Smith's* [Online] Available at: https://www.smithsalternative.com/events/geoff-s-jazz-at-smith-s-64433 [Accessed 21 July 2025].

Solly, B., 2012. *Absolute Beginnings* [Online] Available at: https://recordcollectormag.com/articles/absolute-beginnings [Accessed 19 July 2025].

Spillett, S., 2017. *The Long Shadow of the Little Giant*. 2nd ed. Sheffield: Equinox.

Spillett, S., 2021. *The Old Ching-Ching-Ching* [Online] Available at: https://www.simonspillett.com/blog/the-old-ching-ching-ching.aspx [Accessed 22 July 2025].

Spotify, n.d. *Australian All-Stars* [Online] Available at: https://open.spotify.com/artist/3E7JshISOPTSHskiqAM22Y [Accessed 21 July 2025].

Starlite International, 1989. *Six O'Clock Rock, the Facts*. Liverpool, New South Wales: Starlite International Pty Ltd.

Sterne, T., 1959. Sydney Spotlight. *Music Maker*, April, p. 31.

Sutherland, K., 2008. Top Jazz Trio at Conservatorium: Classics. *Newcastle Herald*, 17 July, p. 32.

Sutton, K., 2016. *Mike Nock Trio's Smooth Jazz Arrives at QPAC* [Online] Available at: https://scenestr.com.au/music/mike-nock-trio-s-smooth-jazz-arrives-at-qpac [Accessed 21 July 2025].

Swank, 1949. The Jig Rhythm Club. *The 45 Club News*, 15 October, p. 2.

Sydney Jazz Club, 1957. Advertisement. *Australian Jazz Quarterly*, April (31), p. 19.

Taylor, R., 1966. Blowing Hot and Cold. *The Bulletin*, 88(4530), p. 18.

Teenager's Weekly, 1960. Backed Blues – and Won. *Teenager's Weekly*, 8 June, p. 7.

The Age, 1959a. Embers. *The Age*, 4 August, p. 8.

The Age, 1959b. AW Jazz Session from Nightclub. *The Age Radio & Television Supplement*, 4 September, p. 2.

The Age, 1959c. 500 Escape from Blazing Night Club. *The Age*, 9 November, p. 3.

The Age, 1959d. Thursday Television – ABV Channel 2. *The Age Radio & Television Supplement*, 29 October, p. 12.

The Age, 1960. Saturday, December 10. *The Age Radio / TV Supplement*, 8 December, p. 7.

The Age, 1963. Commercial Stations … Monday. *The Age TV-Radio Guide*, 5 September, p. 9.

The Argus, 1952. Thousands of Items Hit by Import Restrictions. *The Argus*, 10 March, p. 13.

The Australian Music Centre, 2016. *The Mike Nock Trio – Three Out 'Redux': The Classic Move Album Revisited* [Online] Available at: https://www.australianmusiccentre.com.au/event/the-mike-nock-trio-three-out-redux-the-classic-move-album-revisited [Accessed 21 July 2025].

The Australian Music Maker and Dance Band News, 1960. Cover. *The Australian Music Maker and Dance Band News*, June, 6(1), p. cover i.

The Australian Women's Weekly, 1961. Listen Here. *The Australian Women's Weekly*, 28(37), p. 4.

The Bulletin, 1961. Girl with a Mind of Her Own. *The Bulletin*, 4 January, 82(4221), p. 14.

The Canberra Jazz Club, 1961. Advertisement: The Canberra Jazz Club. *The Canberra Times*, 13 March, p. 11.

The Embers, 1959. Advertisement. *The Australian Jewish Herald*, 31 July, p. 4.

The Mirror, 1952. Sport of the Brave. *The Mirror*, 10 May, p. 7.

The National Film and Sound Archive of Australia, 2014. *Opening of the Columbia Graphophone Company by Admiral Sir Dudley de Chair KCB MVO* [Online] Available at: https://www.nfsa. gov.au/collection/curated/asset/96154-opening-columbia-graphophone-company-admiral-sir-dudley-de-chair-kcb [Accessed 19 July 2025].

The New Bogart's, 1981. Advertisement. *Hertfordshire Mercury*, 3 April, p. 49.

The Press, 1961. Three Out Jazz Trio Open Tour in City. *The Press*, 18 April, p. 15.

The Sacramento Bee, 1959. People and Places. *The Sacramento Bee*, 9 August, pp. L–17.

The San Francisco Examiner, 1968. Quartet to Make Debut. *The San Francisco Examiner*, 16 August, p. 29.

The Sun-Herald, 1950. 'True Jazz' Fans Meet. *The Sun-Herald*, 24 December, p. 4.

The Sun-Herald, 1961. U.S. Star on ATN 7 Tonight. *The Sun-Herald*, 5 March, p. 23.

The Sydney Morning Herald, 1956a. ABN to Open in November. *The Sydney Morning Herald – ATN Television Supplement*, 15 October, p. 2.

The Sydney Morning Herald, 1956b. T.V. Era Has Started to Change Australians' Way of Life. *The Sydney Morning Herald*, 22 September, p. 2.

The Sydney Morning Herald, 1956c. All Star Week. *The Sydney Morning Herald TV Guide*, 25 November, p. 1.

The Sydney Morning Herald, 1958. Jazz, Classics in the Same Music Club!. *The Sydney Morning Herald*, 1 March, p. 2.

The Sydney Morning Herald, 1959a. Telecast by Jazz Group. *The Sydney Morning Herald TV Guide*, 20 April, p. 2.

The Sydney Morning Herald, 1959b. Variety Program Changes. *The Sydney Morning Herald TV Guide*, 24 April, p. 1.

The Sydney Morning Herald, 1959c. Coffee Lounge Emptied by Smoke Bomb. *The Sydney Morning Herald*, 14 February, p. 1.

The Sydney Morning Herald, 1959d. Stadium Show 'A Gasser' to 10,000 Fans. *The Sydney Morning Herald*, 25 July, p. 11.

The Sydney Morning Herald, 1959e. Guard for Fabian at Show. *The Sydney Morning Herald*, 17 October, p. 25.

The Sydney Morning Herald, 1960a. New £145,000 Wiley Park Hotel Opened. *The Sydney Morning Herald*, 15 March, p. 26.

The Sydney Morning Herald, 1960b. 20,000 Crowd Watches Rock'n'roll Shows. *The Sydney Morning Herald*, 23 January, p. 11.

The Sydney Morning Herald, 1961. Jazz Special. *The Sydney Morning Herald TV Guide*, 6 February, p. 1.

The Sydney Morning Herald, 1987. Radio. *The Sydney Morning Herald – The Guide*, 23 March, p. 13.

The Toowoomba Chronicle, 1961. Week-end Television Programmes. *The Toowoomba Chronicle*, 1 April, p. 7.

The University of Melbourne, 2006. *History of Jazz in Australia. (AHS 05 – 2 CDs) with 59-Page Booklet* [Online] Available at: https://webarchive.nla.gov.au/awa/20060901113001/ http://www.music.unimelb.edu.au/research/CSAM/jazz.html [Accessed 21 July 2025].

Thompson, D., 2002. New Zealand's Rock King, Johnny Devlin. *Goldmine*, 28(583), p. 59.

Tomes, S., 2024. *Women and the Piano: A History in 50 Lives*. New Haven, CT: Yale University Press.

Tomkins, L., 1966. Part Two of Music & Moore. *Crescendo*, August, p. 18.

Trueman, L., 2025. *Heritage Data Form: 80 Oxford Street, Woollahra* [Online] Available at: https://hdp-au-prod-app-woollahra-yoursay-files.s3.ap-southeast-2.amazonaws.com/4917/4461/0862/Oxford_Street_and_Centennial_Flats_Heritage_Assessment_Inventory_80_Oxford_St_WOOLLAHRA.pdf [Accessed 11 August 2025].

Tubby Hayes Band, T., 2009. *BBC Jazz for Moderns* [Sound Recording] (Gearbox Records).

Tudor, R., 1961. Australia. *The Cash Box*, 22(28), p. 48.

Twentsch Dagblad Tubantia, 1952. Zeven keer 'Butch'a me' – Pia Beck Is Niet 'Wild' Op Boogie-Woogie. *Twentsch Dagblad Tubantia*, 10 October, p. 9.

Vagg, S., 2023. *Rock'n'Roll Is Back Again* [Online] Available at: https://www.filmink.com.au/rocknroll-is-back-again/ [Accessed 8 September 2025].

Value Your Music, 2008. *Vinyl: Sittin' In with the 3 Out Lp Australian Jazz M.nock* [Online] Available at: https://www.valueyourmusic.com/items/130274967828-sittin-in-with-the-3-out-lp-australian-jazz-m-nock [Accessed 26 July 2025].

Value Your Music, 2009. *Vinyl: The 3 Out Move Mega Rare Aussie Jazz Lp Mike Nock* [Online] Available at: https://www.valueyourmusic.com/items/220357138195-the-3-out-move-mega-rare-aussie-jazz-lp-mike-nock [Accessed 26 July 2025].

Value Your Music, 2016. *Vinyl: The 3 Out Trio Sittin' In Lp 1961 Oz Jazz 1st Columbia Pressing Mike Nock* [Online] Available at: https://www.valueyourmusic.com/items/182202182783-the-3-out-trio-sittin-in-lp-1961-oz-jazz-1st-columbia-pressing-mike-nock [Accessed 26 July 2025].

Value Your Music, 2020. *Vinyl: Rare Emi Columbia Australian 1st Pressing The 3-Out 'Move' Flipback Lp Jazz Record Extremly Rare /scxo 7505, Laminate Front Flipback Cover* [Online] Available at: https://www.valueyourmusic.com/items/202956517858-rare-emi-columbia-australian-1st-pressing-the-3-out-move-flipback-lp-jazz-record-extremly-rare-scxo-7505-laminate-front-flipback-cover [Accessed 26 July 2025].

van de Leur, W., 2018. The Reception and Development of Jazz in the Netherlands (1945–1970s). In: F. Mehring, H. Bak & M. Roza, eds. *Politics and Cultures of Liberation: Media, Memory, and Projections of Democracy*. Leiden, Netherlands: Koninklijke Brill NV, pp. 177–91.

Van Eyle, W., ed., 1981. *The Dutch Jazz & Blues Discography 1916–1980*. Utrecht: Het Spectrum.

Various, 1960. *1st International Jazz Festival Adelaide 26.10.1960* [Sound Recording] (Australian Jazz Museum).

Various, 1995. *Bodgie Dada & The Cult of Cool* [Sound Recording] (ABC Jazz).

Various, 2003. *Pie Cart Rock'n'Roll* [Sound Recording] (Zerox).

Victor Harbour Times, 1958. Much Travelled Jazz Artist. *Victor Harbour Times*, 24 October, p. 4.

Victorian Jazz Archive, 2013. Important CD Release on the Vjazz Label: Almost Ampersand –The Unissued Bill Miller Recordings. *VJazz* (57), p. 3.

Vinyl Vulture, 2006. *Lead On … Roy Budd* [Online] Available at: https://web.archive.org/web/20060617165131/http://vinylvulture.co.uk/features/roy_budd.php [Accessed 21 July 2025].

Vulture, S., 2006. *Persuasive Percussion – Chris Karan* [Online] Available at: https://web.archive.org/web/20060617165440/http://www.vinylvulture.co.uk/interviews/chris_karan.php [Accessed 19 July 2025].

Wallace, S., 2023. *Interview on Facebook* [Interview] (26 September 2023).

Waples, J., 2024. *Interview by Phone* [Interview] (9 October 2024).

Ward, A., 2012. *'Any Rags, Any Jazz, Any Boppers Today?' Jazz in New Zealand 1920–1955*. Auckland: University of Auckland.

Ward, E., 1961. Jazz Exciting Sunday Session. *Evening Chronicle*, 10 November, p. 6.

Ward, K., 1961. U.S. Scholarship to Aust. Jazz Pianist. *Teenagers' Weekly*, 13 December, p. 4.

Warren, J., 1961. New Zealand Message. *Music Maker*, June, p. 47.

Welding, P., 1989. *Birth of the Cool*. s.l.: Capitol Jazz.

Weldon, N., 2023. *Interview on Facebook* [Interview] (25 September 2023).

Wes, 1968. Jazz Australia. *On Dit*, 36(5), p. 10.

Whitcomb, N., 1950. Under the Counter. *Daily Mirror*, 22 April, p. 6.

Whiteoak, J., 1998. *Playing Ad Lib: Improvisatory Music in Australia 1836–1970*. Sydney: Currency Press.

Whiteoak, J. A., 1985. *Early Modern Jazz in Australia – The Introduction of Bop*. Bundoora, Victoria: Latrobe University.

Whittle, T., 1956. *Spotlighting* [Sound Recording] (Esquire).

Williams, M., 1981. *The Australian Jazz Explosion*. Sydney: Angus & Robertson Publishers.

Wilson, J., 2017. *2017: Try Turning It OFF and ON Again* [Online] Available at: https://julienwilson.com/2017-try-turning-it-off-and-on-again/ [Accessed 26 July 2025].

Wilson, R., 1968. Fine John Handy Quintet Returns. *Oakland Tribune*, 25 May, pp. 5–B.

Wolf Abramowitz, 1958. Advertisement. *The Australian Jewish News*, 11 April, p. 4.

YouTube, 2025. *Music for Your Ears* [Online] Available at: https://www.youtube.com/@MusicForYourEars [Accessed 22 August 2025].

Index

A

Abramowitz, Wolf 18

Adelaide 44–8, 56, 61

Arno, Russ 30, 38, 87

Atwell, Winifred 8–9, 33

Auckland 10–11, 59

Australian All-Stars, The 28–9,
36–9, 42–3, 45, 55, 57, 61,
63–4, 71

'Autumn in New York' 43

B

Bailey, Colin 30, 33–4, 56

Basin Street Jazz Centre 58

Be! Jazz 89–90

Beck, Pia 4–5

Bell, Graeme 16, 27–8, 30,
61

Bennett, Graeme 28

Berklee College of Music 63, 67,
71–2

Bertles, Bob 11–12

Bevan, Cyril 26, 30

Beyond El Rocco 74–5

Bird's Basement 93

Birth of the Cool 5, 41

Blakey, Art 12, 31, 39, 72, 94

Bob Gillette Quartet, The 50

Bob Paris Combo 11

Bodgie Dada & the Cult of Cool
84–6

Brisbane 44–5, 51, 74, 93

Brown, Carl 21–2

Bryce Rohde Quartet 33, 45, 48,
55–7, 82

Budd, Roy 76, 79

Buddle, Errol 15, 60–1

Burrows, Don
pre-1960s 14, 26–8, 30, 37–8,
60–1
1960s 60, 63, 65
1980s–present 74, 87, 98

C

Caddy, Brian 80

Cale, Bruce 32, 36, 70–1

Canberra 58, 93

Canberra Jazz Club 47

Caplice, Pat 25–7, 37, 39, 55,
57, 87

Christchurch 7, 59

Christie, Keith 7

Clare, John 84

Clare, Kenny 81

Clarke, Bruce 51

Clarke, Kenny 67

Clay, Sonny 13–14

Cole, Nat 'King' 10, 44

Cool School of the 1950s, The
86–7

Cooper, Johnny 10

D

Dankworth, Johnny 7, 69

Davis, Miles 5, 18, 35, 39–41,
46, 59

Deuchar, Jimmy 7, 69
Devlin, Johnny 10–11, 65
Down Beat 60, 63

E
Edwards, Bruce 32
El Rocco
    1950s 12, 30–1
    1960s 32–6, 43, 49–50, 53,
        56, 58, 62–4, 82, 84, 93, 99
    1980s–90s 74–5
Embers, The 19, 21–5, 41, 84
Embers Quintet, The 22, 39,
        55, 57
EMI 38, 67, 86, 89, 97

F
Fabulous Flamingos, The 10
Falson, Ron 14, 16, 26, 60–3, 66
First Australian International
        Jazz Festival 44–9, 64, 84,
        97, 99
First World War 13
Flamingo, The 6, 10, 68
Flamingo Restaurant, The 18
Fochi, Sergio 17–18
Foundry616, 92
Fourth Way, The 73–4
Frank Thornton Quintette 21–2
Freddy Logan's All Stars 28
'Freshwater' 42, 47, 53, 57, 71, 94

G
Gardiner, Gerry 12
Gebert, Bobby 35
Getz, Stan 21
Gillespie, Bruce 51
Gillespie, Dizzy 3, 9, 15, 45–8, 56

Gillett, Bob 12, 50
Gold, Jan 26
Gordon, Lee 43–5, 48–9, 56, 61,
        64–5, 84
Gottschalk, Micha 89, 97
Graham, Kenny 4, 6

H
Hawkins, Coleman 2–4, 45–6
Hayes, Tubby 7, 68–71, 76, 81
Hibbler, Al 45
Hirst, Brett 92
History of Jazz in Australia 86,
        97
Hungry I, The 49–50

I
'If I Were a Bell' 40, 95

J
James, Arthur 30–1
Jazz At The Embers 22, 39, 55
Jazz Centre 44, 17
Jazz Club 11, 25–6, 28, 62, 64
Jazz for Beach-Niks 29, 36–7,
        85
Jazz for Beach-Niks Volume 2, 29,
        37, 42, 57
Jazz for Pleasure 28
Johnson, Bruce 34, 84
Johnson, J.J. 21
Jonah Jones Quartet 45
Jones, Colin 12, 31, 34, 60, 62

K
Kelly, Catherine 79
Kennedy, Ian 49–50
Knowles, Jimmy 22, 24

L
Laird, Rick 35, 50, 60, 63, 70
Langlands, Paula 58–60
Lee, Sammy 24–5
Lee, Sharon 49–50
Levy, Dave 35
Liepolt, Horst 17–18, 34
'Little Niles' 42, 47, 54, 58–9,
        86–7, 97
Loganberries, The 30, 38
'Loganberries' 62, 66
Loggen, John F. 7
London 2, 6, 65, 67–71, 79

M
Make Ours Music 29
McDaniels, Gene 45, 48–50
McGann, Bernie 11
Meadmore, Clement 31, 53
Melbourne
     pre-1960s 12, 17–19, 21,
        25
     1960s 41–2, 44–5, 47, 58
     2010s 92
Mike Nock Orchestra, The 30
Millers, The 2, 4
Mingus, Charles 9
Moore, Dudley 68–9, 76–7, 79,
        83
'Move' 5, 41, 47
'Music Maker' 1957 All Stars, The
        21, 27–8, 38–9, 87

N
Nettelbeck, Ted 54, 70
Ngaruawahia 7

O
O'Keefe, Johnny 11–12, 29, 44,
        64–5, 75
Osborne, Don 25

P
Page, Geoff 93–4
Parker, Charlie 4, 9, 21, 43
Peace, Arthur 8
Peterson, Oscar 41–3, 53
Pigalle Theatre Restaurant 48,
        84
Pochée, John 11
Powell, Bud 9, 17, 67
Powell Twins, The 30
Power, Lucille 5–7
Primitif, The 43, 49
'Primitive' 40, 87, 95

Q
QPAC Cremorne Theatre 93

R
Reeves, Wilmus 21–3
Revue 61, 58
Rex Hotel 25, 33
RHMS *Patris* 63
Roach, Max 9, 41
Ruteledge, Dave 26

S
Scott, Ronnie 7, 65, 67–8, 70–1,
        80
Second World War 1–2, 14
Sheraton Skyline 79–80
Silver, Horace 17, 39

Sittin' In 61–2, 65–6, 82, 85, 91,
    97
Six O'Clock Rock 29, 51, 58
Sky Lounge 28–9, 43, 51, 64–5
Sloggett, Jimmie 32, 37
Smith, Derek 6
Smith, Frank 21, 24
Smith's Alternative 93–5
'Softly as in a Morning Sunrise'
    41, 47
Some Jazz in Australia 48
Speer, Stewart 12
'Squeeze Me' 39, 94
Staton, Dakota 45, 48, 70–1
'Strictly from Hunger' 37
Surfers Paradise 18
Sydney
    pre-1960s 7, 11–14
    1960s 24–6, 28–32, 34, 44–8,
        51, 56, 59–65, 75, 82,
        84–5
    2000s 91–3

T
Taylor, Art 67
Teddy Wilson Trio 45, 48
Temperley, Joe 7
Thornton, Frank 12, 18–19, 21–2
Three Out Redux, The 92–5
Trask, Diana 43–4

V
Vaughan, Sarah 45, 48
'Velvet Waters' 51
Virgil, Barbara 21–3, 48

W
Waples, James 92, 95
'Way Back' 40–1, 81, 85–6
Webber, Ron 28
Wellington 10, 48, 59
Weston, Billy 22–3
Whittle, Tommy 6–7, 43, 69
Wilkinson, Terry 28, 41, 54, 63
Wilson, Nancy 50